Charles Minnigerode

Sermons by the Rev. Charles Minnigerode

Charles Minnigerode

Sermons by the Rev. Charles Minnigerode

ISBN/EAN: 9783337159665

Printed in Europe, USA, Canada, Australia, Japan

Cover: Foto ©Lupo / pixelio.de

More available books at **www.hansebooks.com**

SERMONS

BY THE

REV. CHARLES MINNIGERODE, D. D.,

RECTOR OF ST. PAUL'S CHURCH, RICHMOND, VA.

RICHMOND:
WOODHOUSE & PARHAM
1880.

PREFACE.

This volume is published at the earnest request and by the kindness of a few members of my congregation. In the selection of the sermons, I have been guided in part by the wishes of my friends. They are sent forth in the humble hope, that in them one more testimony is published to the truth of the Gospel and the blessed revelation of Christ and Him crucified.

Owing to the fact that I insisted upon being my own corrector of the proof-sheets, a few errors have remained in these pages. The following list contains the few which might interfere with the thorough understanding of the text:

ERRATA.

Page 22, line twenty-two, *degradations*, read *degradation*.
Page 56, line eleven, *apostles*, read *Apostle*.
Page 63, lines four and eleven, *one*, read *One*.
Page 69, line penultimate, *immoral*, read *immortal*.
Page 80, line two, "*All this,*" read "*All this is thine!*"
Page 120, line fifteen, punctuate "*manifestations. But,*" &c., line eighteen, "*our creed: a true,*" &c.
Page 147, line eighteen, *over*, read *even*.
Page 283, line eleven, "*inate*," read "*innate.*"

CONTENTS.

PAGE.

I. THE ALL OF MAN 1–14

"The thing that hath been, it is that which shall be; and that which is done, is that which shall be done; and there is no new thing under the sun."—*Ecclesiastes* i. 9.

II. WHAT SHALL IT PROFIT? 15–26

"What shall it profit a man if he gain the whole world. and lose his own soul?"—*Mark* viii. 36.

III. WHAT THEN? 25–43

"And he confessed, and denied not; but confessed, I am not the Christ. And they asked him, What then?"—*John* i. 20, 21.

IV. THE NAME OF CHRISTIAN 44–60

"The Disciples were called Christians first at Antioch."—*Acts* xi. 26.

V. THE BREAD OF LIFE 61–75

"Man shall not live by bread alone, but by every word that proceedeth out of the mouth of God."—*Matthew* iv 4.

VI. FORBIDDEN FRUIT 76–89

"In the day that thou eatest thereof, thou shalt surely die."—*Genesis* ii. 17.

VII. WEIGHED IN THE BALANCES . . . 90–104

"Tekel—thou art weighed in the balances, and art found wanting."—*Daniel* v. 27.

VIII. REPENT 104–118

"The times of this ignorance God winked at, but now commandeth all men everywhere to repent."—*Acts* xvii. 30.

CONTENTS.

IX. No God 119-138

"The fool hath said in his heart, there is no God."—*Psalms* xiv. 1.

X. Fruits 139-153

"What fruit had ye then in those things, whereof ye are now ashamed? for the end of those things is death."—*Romans* vi. 21.

XI. Satisfied 154-166

"I shall be satisfied when I awake with thy likeness."—*Psalms* xvii. 15.

XII. Press Toward the Mark 167-180

"Brethren, I count not myself to have apprehended: but this one thing I do, forgetting those things which are behind, and reaching forth unto those things which are before, I press toward the mark for the prize of the high calling of God in Christ Jesus." *Philippians* iii. 13, 14.

XIII. Count the Cost 181-195

"Which of you intending to build a tower sitteth not down first and counteth the cost, whether he have sufficient to finish it?"—*Luke* xiv. 28.

XIV. Lost by Hope 196-208

"We are saved by hope."—*Romans* viii. 24.

XV. Perfecting Holiness . . . 209-223

"Having, therefore, these promises, dearly beloved, let us cleanse ourselves from all filthiness of the flesh and spirit, perfecting holiness in the fear of God."—*II. Corinthians* vii. 1.

XVI. God's Saving and Ours 224-238

"I am thine—save me."—*Psalms* cxix. 94.
"Work out your own salvation!"—*Philippians* ii. 12.

XVII. Obedience 239-252

"Whatsoever he saith unto you, do it."—*John* ii. 5.

CONTENTS.

XVIII. Two Masters 253–265

"No man can serve two masters."—*Matthew* vi. 24.

XIX. God's Holy Temple 266–280

"The Lord is in his holy temple."—*Psalms* xi. 4.—*Habakkuk* ii. 20.

XX. The Incarnation 281–301

"God, who, at sundry times and in diverse manners, spake in times past unto the fathers by the prophets, has, in these last days, spoken to us by His Son."—*Hebrews* i. 1, 2.

XXI. Communion Sermon 302–311

"What have I to do any more with idols?"—*Hosea* xiv. 8.

SERMONS.

The thing that hath been, it is that which shall be; and that which is done, is that which shall be done; and there is no new thing under the sun.

ECCLES. i. 9.

The Book from which the text is taken is one of peculiar and painful interest. There is a voice of wailing passing through its leaves, a key-note of sadness intonating its every strain. It is the recantation of the wisest among men, of the follies and errors into which the supposed greatness and hoped for satisfaction of this world had led him. And in the sadness which seems to dim his eye, as he glances over his past life and finds all his gains a blank; in the sorrow which I fancy thickens the voice of the Royal Preacher, as he contrasts the eager pursuits and dazzling scenes of his former life with the lesson of disappointment and sense of vacancy they left behind, I find a depth of poetry which is akin to the elegiac pathos of the Romance. The melancholy which breathes through the pages of the great Scottish Poet, and which gives them that power of fascination with which it entranced our youthful imagination, arises from the consciousness of the writer that he dwells on men and times which are gone and can never return; from the longing of his mind to flee from the empty present, and relieve its prosy reality with the reproduction of the heroic forms of the Crusaders, or the sacrifices of chivalrous loyalty in the death-struggle of the house of Stuart. Wonderful and mysterious is the power with which the reputed poems of Ossian move us: but that power lies less in the words we read, than in the image they bring to our minds of the desolate son of Fingal, the last of his race, striking his lonely harp and chanting the requiem over the loved forms and the days of glory that had passed with the mighty dead of his family; and which in its native wildness comes to us like the echo of the wind that sighed over their resting-place, and swept through the fir-trees that shaded them, as through gigantic strings of the æolian harp.

But a greater than a poet is here: the sage of Juda, the great king of Israel, who had lived what others could but sing of. When I read this Book, and see the monarch, in whom dwelt all the fulness of earthly majesty, leave his throne; see the philosopher, who surpassed by his wise sayings all the children of men, turn from his books; see the possessor of wealth which Ophir poured into his lap and the ships of Tarshish brought to his treasury, famished mid golden dust; see the man that had exhausted all the sources of earthly joy, and tasted every human pleasure, sickened with disappointment; when I see Solomon, the great, the admired, the wise and prosperous, look over the monuments of his brilliant career, and write upon them all, upon his throne and regal power, his life-long labours, his riches and his untold pleasures—"Vanity! vanity of vanities! all is vanity!!" I learn that here I have more than a fleeting poem—an epitaph on all human greatness; more than the plaintive cry of farewell—a lamentation over the vanity of every earthly pursuit; more than vain regrets over the past—the stern lesson of a life, whose reality surpassed the wonders of fiction: that all that this earth can give does not minister satisfaction to the immortal soul; but that, having roamed through every department of human life, and climbed every height of human grandeur, and searched every depth of human wisdom, and ransacked every means of human enjoyment, he finds them all a weariness and vexation of spirit, and learns that godliness alone, that religion alone, can speak peace, and give lasting satisfaction to the restless and aspiring heart; that the whole matter, *the all of man*, is to "fear God and keep his commandments." "For God shall bring every work into judgment, with every secret thing, whether it be good, or whether it be evil."

In truth I never read this Book, but I hear the accompaniment of the spirit's voice, which now whispers to me with affectionate solicitude, "Love not the world, nor the things that are in the world," and again, with the deep notes of warning, as with a funeral knell, breaks on my ear: "Be ye also ready; for in such an hour as ye think not, the Son of Man cometh."

The epitome of the wise man's experience is contained in the words of the text—"The thing that hath been, it is that which shall be; and that which is done is that which shall be done; and there is no new thing under the sun."

1.—"The thing that hath been, it is that which shall be."

Life is the same it has ever been, and always will be, and its experience is the same. Even the practical unbelief in this truism, of which we all are guilty, attests its universality. The delusion of life consists in its promise of happiness and satisfaction, with which it charms the natural man into its bondage—at last to pay him off with disappointment! It ever conjures up some phantom which he pursues and never reaches; or, if he reaches it, finds that like Ixion, he embraced a shadow! In vain that past experience teaches this lesson. In vain that the world with one voice attests the instability and deceitfulness of earthly hopes; that they who have reached the goal proclaim in mournful tones that it was not worth the race. Man clings to the delusion, and foolishly hopes that, whatever be the experience of others, he shall obtain its promises. There is not a child in our families here present but fancies that as soon as he shall arrive at a certain stature he shall enjoy more pleasure than he has enjoyed in his childhood. And there is not a man of years before me but looks back to the days of his childhood as the only season of paradisical happiness which has fallen to his lot. The youth aspires to a settled life; the active man to obtain, after labour and toil, a state of rest and satisfaction; but the lesson must be learned by all, that rest belongs not to the present moment, and satisfaction does not crown their earthly aspirations!

"The thing that hath been, it is that which shall be!" The experience of man is the same now as it was in the days of the Psalmist; his "life is labour and sorrow, so soon passeth it away and we are gone." And, standing amidst the wreck of all his hopes and aspirations, amidst the joys which in vain he had sought to taste, the broken toys with which in vain he had tried to cheat himself into happiness, he repeats the despairing cry of the preacher: "Vanity! all is vanity and vexation of spirit!"

I have seen the young man, buoyant with hopes, and his heart swelling with proud aspirations. But before they could ripen into fruit, or even open into the blossom, the blight of this life had fallen upon them, and desolation seized his soul! How many of your hopes have been realized? How many of your fondest desires crowned with success? How many of your loftiest flights succeeded, your sternest resolves been carried out? Who is there among you, young or old, who stand precisely where they expected to stand, to whom life has brought what they asked for and sought after? Who, among those who have reached the years of manhood, had not to come down from the pinnacle of bliss and glory, which in younger years they fancied they were climbing, and which their youthful dreams had held up to their imagination, and been forced to content themselves with the beggarly gifts of real life?

I have seen the student go with thirsting soul to the fountains of knowledge, and pore day and night over the volumes of ancient lore, and labour hard to master the mysteries of science. I looked again, and saw him vainly slake his thirst in the muddy streams of error and hopeless speculation, and the wrinkles on his brow attested that "in much wisdom there is much grief," and that "he that increaseth knowledge increaseth sorrow!"

I have seen the warrior, bearing the banner of victory from land to land. I looked again, and saw him, Alexander-like, weep that he had no more worlds to conquer; or, bound to a sea-girt St. Helena, chafe in his exile, and mourn over the passing nature of all earthly glory!

I have seen the monarch, glorying in regal pride, and courtiers bowing lowly, and nations taxed for his pleasure. I looked again, and saw him tremble on the throne, the Damocles sword suspended over him; or saw him, a fugitive, banished from his home, and "none so poor as to do him reverence!"

I have seen the statesman, rising on the tide of popular favor, and seize the highest honors of the country. I looked again, and saw how cares had followed him; or saw him dashed from his lofty position by the first storm that turned the fickle multitude.

I passed the stately mansion, gorgeous with wealth and replete with all that can charm the eye and please the taste, and minister comfort. I entered, and saw its owner stretched on the bed of lingering, and envying the poor at his door for one hour of health, and a portion of his strength.

I have seen the rich who trusted in his riches,

with treasures in his possession that could have relieved a starving multitude, with gold at his command that crowded his house with flatterers, and made him the idol of hungry dependants. I looked again, and the riches had made themselves wings and were gone; or the craven wretch was watching his coffers with the line of care upon his brow, and fear in his eye; or, starving amidst his hoarded wealth, still thirsting for more, and cry "give, give!"

I have tasted the joys of earth, and seen the gay and the reveller. I looked again, and in that wan form, and ennui of life, I saw that this too is vanity!

I have visited the family circle, and seen the peaceful fireside, and the children like olive branches wreathing the table. I looked again, and there was the vacant chair, that told the story of that stifled sob and those weeping eyes.

I looked upon beauty, and a few summers dimmed the radiant eye, and faded the blushing roses. I have looked upon youth, and I saw the spoiler drawing near, steadily, certainly, to break its strength and extinguish its glow.

I have looked upon life in all its forms—like a splendid phantasmagoria it passed before my eye—but all its moments are fleeting, all its glory "passing away!" In the experience of the past we have the horoscope of the future. Six thousand years have taught us that "the thing that has been, it is that which shall be."

II. Ah, life is indeed a phantasmagoria. We scarcely view it but it passes away; passes away, brethren, into an endless future. Its shadows recede, and give way to the realities of eternity! But that eternity of the creature *begins here*, and its law is written in our text: "that which is done, is that which shall be done;" what is done *here* shall be done *there*.

"Whatsoever a man soweth, that shall he also reap." "He that soweth to the flesh shall of the flesh reap corruption; and he that soweth to the spirit shall of the spirit reap life everlasting." As certain as the crop of the husbandman will be of the seed he has put in the ground, so shall man, when once put under the green sod of God's acre, grow up in eternity, the same in tendencies, desires, thoughts.

The same? Yet not the same! For in this new existence, when the living soul is less confined by the narrow limits, and less weighed down by the heavy material of this earthly body; when the flight of his thoughts, and the impetuosity of his desires are less checked by the disturbances and fluctuations, less broken by the attractions and repulsions of this abode of change and unsteadiness; his feelings, thoughts, affections, will be raised to an infinite power, and carry with them their inherent rewards of happiness or misery, as with an almighty force. All holy affections, all kind and charitable feelings, will enlarge themselves without bounds to make us meet companions for Him who is perfect Himself, and calls His creatures to perfection. The modest bud of peace and joy below will open into the full bloom of celestial blessedness! But the embers of sin, if not quenched in this life, will be kindled into flames, ever strengthening in their overpowering sway, ever increasing in the torment they bring with them; yet never dying, never destroying. Lust and hatred and avarice, rising in greediness and vehemence, will find no object to lay their hands of destruction on, but the soul itself which submitted to their dominion here below.

Solemn truth: "The thing that is done is that which shall be done." Oh, what a revelation of Eternity! Are you prepared, my un-Christian brother, to have your slavery to ambitious aims continued in the world to come, in a never-ceasing Sisyphean labor? To let the thirst for earthly pleasure place you, Tantalus-like, before the waters of rejoicing and the fruits of satisfaction, and yet to suffer the thirst and hunger of Eternity! Ye who devote your all to the grovelling pursuits of time that never come to an end, are ye prepared "in the hereafter" to continue the fruitless labour, like the fabled daughters of Danaus, filling the bottomless urn with the draughts of refreshing?

The happiness and perfection of the good will indeed advance forever; the wretchedness and downfall of the wicked will go on forever, and may go on forever in an increasing ratio! Ages of a heavenly existence open new and greater stores of beatitude; more glorious revelations of the Divine nature to the saints; and the wrath of God endured for ages will still be "wrath to come!"

For "that which is done, shall be done again." Here in this life are the premises and conditions of the life to come: "Where the tree falleth, there it shall lie." "He that is unjust, let him be unjust still; he which is filthy, let him be filthy still; he that is righteous, let him be righteous still; and he that is holy let him be holy still."

And what—if this alternative is placed before him, and such the issues of this life—what, then, are all the pains and sorrows of this transient state to him, who knows his home in heaven! who lays up treasures there, and has the promise of Him who is faithful, and by faith receives even here the earnest of an inheritance which passeth not away? And what are all the pleasures, and all the enticements, and the golden chains, with which sin surrounds and binds us here, to him who looks beyond and has "respect to the recompense of reward?"

But oh, the unbeliever! the ungodly! Like that pale, that unhappy poet of our land—whose every hope was in the past, and whose presence bore no flower of happiness; who vainly sought nepenthe for his sufferings; "whom unmerciful disaster followed fast and followed faster," till his song one burden bore,—

> "Till the dirges of his hope one melancholy burden bore
> Of never—nevermore!"

whose nightly vision was disturbed by the croaking voice of the bird of destiny which answered to all his pleas, the hopeless word of "*nevermore!*"—like him he vainly asks of his gods:

> "Tell me truly, I implore,—
> Is there, is there balm in Gilead? tell me, tell me,
> I implore!"—

But the echo returns only the raven's bitter cry of "nevermore!"

III. Alas, brethren, "*there is no new thing under the sun!*" This earth, Antaeus-like, cannot revive your strength; there is no power under the sun which can restore you to that bliss which must be sought without sin! All your schemes of reform, all your proud resolutions cannot raise you into God's favor. All your sacrifices, all your rites, all your superstitions, all your charities, cannot restore in you the image of God, and change the cursed ground into an Eden! There is no stream that purls up from the earth in which to wash our sins away, and draw draughts of renewal: "there is no new thing under the sun." There is no salvation!—unless from above the sun, from the Father of Light, from the fountains of the upper sanctuary, flows down upon you the flood of healing, the stream of salvation! unless God Himself bares His holy arm to bring life and immortality to light; unless you are born again of the spirit, unless a new heart is given you, through the grace of Christ!

Oh, that I had the power of speech, and the gift of persuasion! Oh, that the angel of God would touch my lips, and give me words of fire! Believe me; believe one who has as vile a heart, and passions strong as yours; one who has roamed far and wide to satisfy the yearnings of a selfish and unsubdued spirit; who has drunk deep of the cup of life, and tasted its sorrows and its delights; one who has too many recollections left him of the world not to understand its fashion and the power of its influence; and yet has been taught the vanity of all, and the bitterness of his own heart. Believe me; and, if you will not believe a fellow-sinner, believe Solomon, who rises above us in the knowledge of all that this world can give and bring, and the acquaintance with its every source of strength, and comfort, and pleasure, and happiness, as a Patagonian giant among mere pigmies! And if you will not believe one that could fall as low as Solomon, believe one "greater than Solomon;" one who was "holy, harmless, undefiled and separate from sinners,"—that there is no healing balm except in the Gospel; that there is no peace except in Christ; that the infinite yearnings and aspirations of man can never be satisfied; that his doubts, and the riddles of his earthly existence can never be solved; that the fears of an awakened conscience can never be quieted, except in the religion of the Atonement; and that there is no happiness for man, no lasting joy and bliss and hope, but in the faith and love of Christ, in the pursuit of holiness, and the obedience to the law of God.

And may God have mercy upon you, that now, ere the evil days come, and the years draw nigh when ye shall say "we have no pleasure in them," ye may learn the conclusion of the whole matter:—

"Fear God and keep His commandments, for this is the all of man.

"For God shall bring every work into judgment, with every secret thing, whether it be good, or whether it be evil!"

What shall it profit a man if he gain the whole world, and lose his own soul?

MARK, viii. 36.

THIS is a startling question, brethren, and startling the more as it is asked by Him who made both the world and the soul, and therefore is best able to judge of their relative worth. The manner of the question itself leaves no doubt on the mind which of the two God considers most valuable; and by the sacrifice He made for the soul of man, He showed that He esteemed it above all else, and knew no other price for its worth but His own blood!

And all men know the worth of the soul well enough; but they do not consider its worth sufficiently to let it influence their life! There is, in this respect, the same difference which exists with regard to every point of Religion—the difference between Knowledge and Wisdom, which is drawn occasionally in the Bible; between theory and its practical application. Men know enough of Christ and his redemption, but they do not possess the wisdom to act accordingly. You all know the worth of the soul; may God give you the wisdom to act up to your knowledge.

The Soul! Who can doubt its worth? "Show me the soul," said a skeptic to me; "let me see it, that I may learn to value it, and know it is no mere phantom of the brain; no flattering unction falsely laid to the heart." Can inconsistency go farther? *The Soul!* It beams in that eye which is bent on you in love; it lives in that hand which presses yours in affection; it weeps those tears which are shed over your departed friend; it soars in that thought which compasses the Universe, and reads the laws of the Creator; it yearns for immortality in that uplifted countenance; it dreams of a bliss, and dwells on a happiness for which this earth, and the clay in which it is shrouded on earth, give no satisfaction; it seeks its equals in the realms above, and holds communion with beings as invisible to the natural eye as is its own essence!

Show me its worth! The Creator but spake the word; and earth, fire, water, air, with their countless organizations, burst forth into existence from the womb of Nothing. But when God created man, He took counsel with Himself, in the recesses of the Holy Trinity, and said: "Let us make man in our own image!" On the soul is impressed *the image of God!* who is a Spirit, and can only be known and worshipped in spirit and in truth. *Show me its worth!* Look upon the temple which God built it in the flesh, the noblest work of physical creation; with the brow turned heavenward, and the stature erect, all symmetry, all beauty, such as shines in nothing else! Rehearse its capacities, and see how it compasses the Universe, and moulds Nature to its will, and carves out for itself a way of life, and seeks a happiness to satisfy demands which cannot rise in inert matter! Time does not exhaust its aspirations; life does not set bounds to its desires; it rises above the drudgery of flesh and blood, and seeks its kindred in the heavens! It grasps the idea of God, and rises to the union and communion with the Deity; it rises as on eagle's wings; and in the conception of poets, the thoughts of philosophers, the acquirements of knowledge, gives proof of its heaven-born descent! It is enthroned above the visible creation, the master of this globe, the measurer of the worlds above; and all the treasures of the deep, all the glories of the firmament, all the wonders of science and literature, cannot satiate its appetite, or exhaust its powers. It demands eternity for its progress, infinitude for its development!

It is the soul, alone, brethren, which makes man what he is—*a candidate for eternity!* and oh, either for eternal bliss, or eternal misery! It is the treasure enclosed in the casket of flesh and blood, watched over by powerful spirits, whether for good or evil.

Two worlds are contending for it, and offering their prices for its gain!

There is in this life a contest going on between the powers of Heaven and the powers of Hell. The object of contention is the *soul of man*. God stoops down from Heaven, and bids for the soul; Satan, from beneath, offers his prices for the same.

Whose offer will you take?

Behold from His radiant throne, and the choirs of adoring angels, the Son of God descends, and pleads in accents of love: *Give me thy soul!* I have come for it to earth, and borne the sufferings of the creature. I have borne the form of a servant, and poured out my blood in the death of ignominy, to purchase for it the glories of eternity and the favour of God, who is life; and His loving kindness, which is better than life. Heaven is yours, and eternal joys, which eye hath not seen, nor ear heard, neither have entered into the heart of man to conceive, if you but give me your soul!

Oh, in love He pleads, in love which passeth understanding; and a *price* he offers, the worth of which eternity shall be too short to exhaust. *Heaven* for the soul! *God's presence* for the soul! the *love* of a dying Redeemer and everliving Saviour for the soul! The care and protection of Him in whom we live, and move, and have our being here below; support and strength in every trial, every warfare; triumph over the adversary; victory over death and the grave, in the passage through the dark valley. Infinitude and ever-growing assimilation to the Godhead, as we pass from the Church militant on earth to the Church triumphant in heaven: *All for the soul!* Ah, brethren, God asks no 'sacrifice but of what would make the soul miserable and contemptible. He does not stint His gifts, and gives you for the soul, both the promise of the life that now is, and of that which is to come. Time and eternity unite their appeals to make you take the offer of your Lord, and trust your souls to Him!

What are the prices which the Tempter offers? Ah, can he speak to you of eternity? *He never does!* for his eternity is one of wretchedness indescribable, where the worm never dieth, and the fire is not quenched! Can he point you to future bliss and satisfaction? *He never does;* his wisdom is to hide the future, and drop before it an impenetrable veil of present cares or joys. *This life*, its glory, its power, its wisdom, its lusts, are his all; for beyond them nothing is found in his gift but *Hell! This life*, its glory, its powers, its wisdom, its lusts, are his baits; the prices he offers for the soul, that stays here but for a moment, and before which the present enjoyment flits by as a dream, and if it leaves its mark, it is *the sting of death!*

This life is one great fair, where men's souls are bought and sold. The Church brings it life and salvation, and offers it without money and without price. The World—that great vanity fair—it offers it the baubles of the moment, the regrets and remorse of an eternity. And still it *bids* for *souls*, and *sells* them to its cruel master. There is a constant bargaining of this kind going on! There is not an ungodly pleasure, not an unrighteous gain, not an impure gratification, not a revengeful satisfaction, *but the soul's blood is paid for it!*

The mind of man ever and anon wakes up to this truth: What are all the fictions which have come down to us from more imaginative ages, and now enchain the attention of the young in fairy tales and oriental stories: of men deeding away their souls for the purse that is never empty, the gratification of never-satiate lusts? What are they but the musings of your own heart, its most hidden secrets and deepest wishes, embodied, incarnated in the fascinating form of parabolical fiction? Those legends about the adepts of the black art, the gold makers, or the lords of every pleasure, with evil spirits at their beck and call; yet who with their blood signed away their soul to the adversary, and whose end was the end of despair, in the loathsome embraces of their former demon servants, and the torments of everlasting fire kindled by their busy agency: what are all, but illustrations of this truth, this actual, everpresent, experimental truth: that man cannot give himself only to the pursuit of the wants, the pleasures and the cares of time, the power, wisdom, glory or shame of earth, without surrendering his soul to Him, in whose presence shall be misery for evermore? Oh, that men's eyes were opened to see how, behind every unholy aspiration, every unrighteous transaction, every godless thought, every lustful indulgence, every act of cruelty or hatred, intemperance, or any wickedness, the Evil Spirit stands, ready to take the soul as his pay for all.

And, brethren, look at his prices! Religion and the favour of God will indeed insure you, not only the glories of eternity, but the real joys of earth. Industry will ever find its support, contentment be always rich, the peace of heart a source of never failing happiness, a conscience void of offence a tower of strength amidst all the trials of earth. But the ways of the transgressor, truly they are hard! You ask wealth of this life, and the destroyer turns in its pursuit your thoughts from God and heaven, and thus ruins your soul! but *does he* give you wealth? How many of those who are without

Christ have gotten wealth? wealth to satisfy their wishes, the wants of their greedy nature? "Give! give!" is the constant cry of the soul, its appeal to the king of the world. But, brethren, there are too many applicants for this glittering idol, and you must be satisfied with toiling for it in the sweat of your brow, and working for it "from morn to noon, from noon to dewy eve," and take the paltry gain which scarcely supports existence. See how the devil pays! Are any of you the richer for being without religion? Any of you the better off on earth for having never bestowed a thought on heaven?

Behold the work is as hard and harder in the service of Satan, and his pay, even here—*it is all a fraud!*

You ask happiness, and seek it at the hands of the world, and court its fickle favours, or debase yourselves in its licentious orgies, and seek satisfaction for the thirst of your soul. And after you have roamed through all the haunts of pleasure, and drained the poisonous dregs of its brimming cup, and wallowed in the mire of beastly degradations, *are you happy? are you satisfied?* Has the Devil kept his promise, when he bade you join his merry band, and tread the flowery path of vice? You ask *satisfaction, lasting pleasure*, but, alas, in his service nought is lasting but misery and torment; and surfeit and remorse follow up every pittance that he pays for your soul.

It is fearful to think how many are thus deceived, how many are thus toiling in the bonds of iniquity. How many are ready to purchase a moment's imperfect gratification with long, long hours of wretchedness and remorse; and consent to give up for such wages the hope of heaven?

Oh, when I see the young man madly turn from the lessons of early piety and godliness, and think it manly to throw himself into the ways and vices of a godless world; when I see the acquirements of earth and time become *its all* to the aspiring mind, and the heaven-born glory of our nature degraded in the service of what cannot satisfy, and its strength wasted for that which must prove its ruin; and when I think of the loving remonstrances which a father or mother may in vain address to them, the ceaseless prayers of a Christian wife or sister, whose fervour has not yet been extinguished by repeated failures—a feeling of awe steals over me. It seems to me I see that soul under the hammer, and hear its reckless possessor offer it at auction to the highest bidder. God offers, Christ offers, the Church bids, friends add their prayers. In vain! The Devil seems to bid higher! One more gratification and the soul is "going;" one more successful bargain, and the soul is "going;" one more promise of earthly lust and glory, and the soul is "going," until, brethren, an invisible, almighty hand brings down the hammer—*the hammer of death!* and, as with the archangel's voice, the bargain is sealed for eternity—*gone!*

The silent grave hides its tale of woe. And others come up to the stand, and the auction of this life goes on; and Hell is peopled with immortal souls for the wretched prices of sin, and lust, and greediness! Oh, God!

Brethren, let us follow that soul under the green sod; let us learn the value of the soul from the experience after death! Ah, perhaps success smiled upon it on earth, and the bargains were pleasing, but what is its judgment then? I got a good situation, or a good business—but lost my soul! I made a large fortune—but lost my soul! I had many friends, but God is my enemy. I lived in pleasure, but now pain is my everlasting portion. I clothed my body gaily, but my soul is naked before God; its bed the lake of fire, its sheet the flame that is not quenched, its fellow the worm that never dieth!

Let us go up and ask at the gate of Heaven! ask the bright spirits in the presence of God, and hear what is of the greatest worth in all God's creation: and in language of adoring gratitude they say, *the soul!* Let us go to the gates of Hell, and ask the suffering demons—what is of the greatest worth in all God's creation? and with the howl of despair they cry, *the soul!* Let us visit the graves of the dead, and call up their spirits, Dives and Lazarus, and hear how both, the one from his blissful rest in Abraham's bosom, the other from his bed of torment in Hell, bear the same testimony to the worth of the soul. And, in the stilly Sabbath-hour, kneel down in your own chamber, and ask yourselves:— "What shall it profit *me* if I gain the whole world, and lose my own soul?"

The world! Far be it from us to underrate its claims. We are called into the world, and have our post assigned in it, as the servants of God; and in all its phenomena we may see the overruling power of God, and learn the lessons of His love and justice. We are called to do good in the world, to bear our brethen's burden, and win their souls with ours for Heaven. We are to glorify God in it, by letting our light shine to His praise, and doing our part in its regeneration.

With the love of Christ in the heart, the world cannot hurt us, but will become for us the wrestling place, where the life of the soul is strengthened, and after having enjoyed in it the bounties of God, and been blessed by its every gift, through the gratitude it has waked in our breast to the Giver of every good and perfect gift, we shall bid it farewell calmly, and in the full assurance that from its vale of sorrow and temptation, and its state of imperfection, we shall rise to the blissful home above, where there shall be no more death, sorrow, crying or pain, and "where God shall wipe away the tears from every eye."

But, *without the love of Christ*, and apart from the salvation of the soul,—*the world!* Ah, surely it cannot be reckoned of more worth than *Christ's blood;* that was God's price for it! And all you seek and gain here, in an ungodly life on earth, is worth no more than the thirty pieces of silver that Judas got, and can purchase nothing better for you than the *field of blood in Hell!* the potter's field in Hell, where the souls of strangers shall find their place of execution. Strangers, for Hell was not built for men, but for devils; strangers, for man was not created for condemnation, but has been called to Heaven by the love of a gracious Redeemer.

Brethren, in the name of my Master, with the authority of my office as His messenger, with the urgency of love and deep concern which only a Christian pastor's heart can realize, I ask you to answer the question:

What shall it profit a man if he gain the whole world, and lose his own soul?

What then ?

JOHN, i. 21.

THE banks of the Jordan were crowded by multitudes that had gathered from Jerusalem and all Judea, and the country round about the sacred stream. The wilderness resounded with the unusual noise of masses hurrying to and fro, and again became strangely silent—more so than in its wonted solitude—as the thousands here assembled listened in breathless attention to the voice of the new Prophet who had risen in their midst. In the wilderness where Elija had stayed so often, and from which at last he stepped into the chariot of fire, and was borne on a whirlwind into heaven: there, with the same austere appearance; like him, in raiment of camel's hair, with a leathern girdle round his loins, eating the locusts and wild honey of the desert; like him, "a voice crying in the wilderness," and startling the depraved generation of his day with the thunder-bolts of God's law: John, the son of Zachariah and Elizabeth, appeared. And around him were poured the wondering masses that had ascended from Jerusalem and Jericho on the south ; that had descended from the lake of Genezereth on the north, and crossed the plain of Esdraelon from the land of Galilee. The priests were there, and scribes, and Levites; the publicans, from their hated posts; the soldiers, whose presence warned the people that the sceptre was departing from Juda; the peasants were gathering there, to hear once more the voice of prophecy, which had been silent for four hundred years. And many must have been their musings and anxious speculations, as they looked upon the man of God, and remembered the promise of the coming Messiah—when, from their midst stepped forth the deputation of the Sanhedrim, and gave utterance to the secret questionings of their hearts, and asked him: "Who art thou?" "He confessed and denied not, but confessed 'I am not the Christ.' And they asked him, '*What then?*'"

Let us leave the house of God, to which the wilderness then was consecrated, the heavens its dome and the leafy cover of the Jordan forest, the never-failing waves of the sacred river flowing by; and John, sent from God, preaching repentance and preparing the way of the Lord—let us leave that scene and look upon *this* house of God, where you are gathered to-day, listening to the preached word. Ah, we need not put the question to the Preacher, "Who art thou?" Many there are, alas, to whom he is still like John in the desert, no more than "a voice crying in the wilderness prepare ye the way of the Lord;" whom he yet must startle from the death of sin and worldliness by the terrors of God's law, and the stern demand, "Repent!" Many too, thank God, who have heard the voice of God's condemning law, and feel the bitterness of their own hearts, and to whom, like John to his disciples, he can say: "Behold the Lamb of God, which taketh away the sin of the world!"

But my object is to turn the question upon you, my beloved brethren. You have come to-day into this house of God, which is a Christian Church; come here and prayed to our Heavenly Father, in the name of Jesus; heard His holy prophecies and promises read—all about Christ; you have come to listen to the preaching of Christ and Him crucified, and I would trust you value such days and the temple of God as the time and the place where, more than any where else, you may hear and see Jesus. It is but natural I should ask the question: Are you Christians?

Are you Christians?
If not, what then?

I know some of you are; I know that perhaps many, if personally addressed, would at least be able to express the modest and the trembling hope that they are Christians. And I believe that more of you—God grant that it may be many—will be Christians by the grace of God, even under the poor preaching you hear from our pulpits. But I am justified in assuming that many—that the majority in our congregations—cannot give an affirmative answer to the question: Are you Christians? And I therefore would ask all such, aye, brethren, whether they have made an outward profession of religion or refused it; I would ask all who have just misgivings as to their title to the name of Christian—I would ask all: If not Christians, what then?

Ah, my brethren, if I were to meet any of you to-morrow, and put this question to you; if I were to sit down by your fireside, or in your closet, with none between us but God, and ask you face to face, and soul to soul, are you a Christian? and then should see the drooping eye, and blushing cheek, and that mournful shake of the head, and averted face, which give but too decidedly an answer; and then put to you my present inquiry: "What then?" I am certain you would be as silent *then* as you are *now*.

I know it is easier to ask this question than to answer it. It is the most unnatural, the strangest thing in the world, if any are not Christians, brethren. What! with the Bible before you, and all its evidences? with the blessings around you which have accompanied Christianity? with the open acknowledgment of its truth and necessity, involved in the support you give to the Church and its ministry, in the respect you show to its ordinances and practices, the regularity with which you listen to its teaching and exhortation—*you not Christians?* with its holy influences all around you, with the proofs of its saving, sanctifying, blissful character in your midst, with its hopes and fears constantly before you—*you not Christians! what then?*

Ye young men, the children perhaps of pious parents, that have been rocked to sleep to the hum of a Christian lullaby; that have been taught the name of Jesus when first your stammering lips could lisp your prayers at your mother's knee. Ye young men and women that were dedicated to the service of Christ in infancy in holy baptism, and trained under the nursing influence of His Church; who owe everything you possess that is of lasting value to Christianity, and are the heirs of all the promises of the Bible; whom every sense of duty, every feeling of honour, should lead into allegiance to your Saviour; whose success and prosperity, even here, is connected with your character as Christians, and to whom life opens the brightest prospect only in proportion to the respect you gain, (and, let me tell every young woman, the graces you obtain,) as followers of the meek and lowly Jesus, "holy, harmless, undefiled and separate from sinners;" ye whom everything urges to a Christian life—the tearful prayers of parents, the remonstrance of friends, the appeals of your country, which would place its hopes in you; the love of your Saviour, who sends His most earnest pleadings, and promises his choicest blessings to you, and beseeches you to remember now your Creator, in the days of your youth: are you Christians? *If not*—if, in spite of all these mercies, all these holy influences, all the hopes set before you, all the calls of infinite love to your hearts—so susceptible even by nature to what is great and noble—if you are not Christians, I ask, *what then?*

Ye parents—oh, heaven! must I address my question to parents? to fathers and mothers, upon whom God has bestowed the sweetest heritage of his favour, the dearest pledges of His love; to whom He has given children, children with immortal souls, that they are to train for Heaven and everlasting bliss, or must otherwise look forward to their eternal ruin! parents on whose souls are bound the precious, never-dying souls of those they love better than their own lives, and whose happiness they would purchase at any sacrifice? Parents, whose precept and example is the great channel through which the blessings of God's covenant descend to them; who must bring them to Christ, and precede them there, or they can have no hope of seeing them happy here and blessed hereafter; or they must be content to endure in their eternal prison of woe, above the worm that never dieth, and the fire that is not quenched, the unutterable agony of seeing the darlings of their soul brought to the same ruin of condemnation and howling despair by their guilt, and being charged by them in hell with having wrought their eternal loss and ruin, by their own neglect and destructive guidance and example! Parents,—are you Christians?—Christians yourselves—for unless you are, how can you lead your children away from the paths of sin and death, and hide them in the saving arms of Christ? Are you Christians? *If not*, if you resist all the appeals which nature and natural affection, duty and reason, and God's word make to you, if you are not Christians, I ask, *what then?*

Ye men of business! whose success in life depends on zeal, and honesty, and prudence; and to whom, here in the Bible, we bring such hopes as should quicken the energies of the dullest; and before whom we lay, in the Gospel, a code of morality which outstrips all other codes of law, and to whom we give, in God's word, maxims of prudence and wisdom which charge all the smartness of the world with folly! ye who know that you owe your security, and your neighbor's trustfulness, and your advantages of peace and prosperity, of culture and civilization, to the influence of Christianity, felt, through the length and breadth of the world, and pervading this community in which you trade and work; to whom we offer in the profession and consistent walk of religion a passport to men's confidence, and a high-road to a lofty and honored position, such as nothing else can procure; aye, more, to whom is herein pledged the favour of God, in whom you live and move and have your being, and on whom in all things,—whether consciously or not, willingly or not, submissively or otherwise—you depend; ye, to whom we bring here, amidst the manifold changes of this life, the fearful suddenness of which but too many experience, a firm ground to stand on and a steadfast anchor to rely on; a comfort and solace in affliction and distress, which you well know the cold heart of the world will never give; and even when all forsake you, a Friend that sticketh closer than a brother, and will prove Himself faithful and true the more you may have to lament the passing nature of everything earthly, and the fickleness of human friendship and favor? *Are you Christians? if not, what then?*

Ye aged! to whom life extends no more joys, and no more promises, and no more hopes; who are bowing under the burden of your years, and whose infirmities grow with every day; before whom is yawning, in the near distance, the grave that shall forever close upon you all the delusive charms and false promises, and forever rob you of all the passing idols of this life; but to whom the religion of Jesus offers an eternity of glory and bliss, and a new life which the grave cannot subdue, and for which death has no sting—tell me, oh, tell me, as ye would not bring your gray hairs with shame and dishonor and fear and sorrow into the grave, tell me, *are ye Christians? if not, what then?*

Oh, that I could put this question before every one among you!

Are you Christians? if not, what then? Are you Heathens? Mohammedans, Jews, Atheists? Are you idolaters, robbers, murderers, thieves? No, brethren, I am not going to make you out worse than you are. I do not charge you with any particular sins—humanly considered; I do not rake up the hidden secrets of your life and act the judge before you. No; I believe all that is good and right of you. I take it for granted that you are honest, truthful, candid, attentive to your duties, kind to your neighbor, liberal to the claims of the Gospel, moved to sympathy and active benevolence when the cry of suffering reaches your ear. I'll admit it gladly, and to a greater degree than you would claim. But, brethren, is it *this?* is it their being honest and kind and charitable and sober and truthful, which keeps any one from being a Christian? No, no! In all this the Christian should stand in the foremost rank. And the more of such dispositions in the heart and such actions in our life we can show, the more the Christian has cause to thank God that "He is working in him to will and to do!"

No! If persons refuse a profession of Christ; if they decline the invitation given in great love and affection; if they are forced to answer why they are not Christians, and say "what then" they are— the answer almost universally received is, that they are sinners! *sinners!* I might say, it argues a sad state of things and shows a fearful confusion of right and wrong, when people are more ready to confess that they are sinners than that they are dishonest, unkind, guilty of any particular charge, the mere outcroppings of the sin within; that they will blush before God rather than before man. But what I have to say here, is this: that if ye are sinners, ye are the very persons who ought to be Christians, and are invited to be Christians. It is to sinners that the Gospel is preached, for sinners that Christ has died, to sinners that a way has been opened into the grace and love of God. What else is the Gospel but pardon and new life to sinners? What was it to Peter when he denied his Lord? to Paul, who styles himself the chief of sinners? what is it to me, in whom Christ has shown forth all long-suffering, to encourage others to trust Him likewise? what is it to any Christians, who are men of like passions with you, who have known as much of sin as you, and still know its power as much or more than you do, but a message of peace and pardon to sinners, and the power of God unto salvation to those who, by nature, were under condemnation, as you are, and in the bondage of sin? No, you are no Christians, not because you are sinners, but because you are—and this is the answer to my question: "what then?"—because you are *unbelieving and impenitent sinners!* There can be no other answer. No sin ever has kept any one out of heaven that would go to Jesus for pardon, and in repentance renounce it! This is the very pith and marrow of the Gospel, and thus only it can be glad tidings to fallen man! "Believe in the Lord Jesus Christ and thou shalt be saved." "If we confess our sins, God is faithful and just to forgive us our sins and to cleanse us from all unrighteousness." If you are clear of these two charges—unbelief and impenitence—then come! God has been gracious to you, for you is the marriage feast prepared!

But—think a moment, brethren—*you unbelieving!* who admit the authority of the Bible, who believe Jesus to be the Son of God, who would resent as insult and indignity the charge of infidelity! *You unbelieving*, who build churches, and support the ministry, and aid in sending the Gospel to others, and constantly avail yourselves of the blessings of Christianity! Oh! is it not strange that such inconsistency should be so common, and that with all the assent of the intellect, and all the concurrence of every better feeling, the heart yet can be settled in unbelief, and resolutely refuse to apply that blood to its salvation which they know and acknowledge alone cleanseth from all sin? But, behold! unbelief is supported by *impenitence*. It is because faith cannot be exercised without repentance that faith goes begging. It is because Christ is a Saviour *from* sin, and not *in* our sins, that His grace is rejected.

Impenitent! It is the most fearful thing, brethren, and if you consider it seriously, the most humiliating thing imaginable, that men should refuse to repent! What! to renounce the devil and all his works? his deeds of darkness and sins of unright-

-eousness and lust, which you would shrink from as before the public eye, so at the forum of your own conscience? To renounce them, brethren, not to say that you have not been, or perhaps are not guilty of them, surely liable to them; but from this moment onward to resolve to give them up, and in the strength of Christ, pledged to you in His own word, which you cannot disbelieve, to resist them. Can you refuse this? To renounce the vain pomp of the world and its vanities? to resolve to give them up rather than Heaven and Christ, who died for you? to renounce the sinful desires of the flesh, which are as leprosy preying upon you here? Can you refuse to renounce them? and refuse obediently to keep God's holy will and commandments? and retain your self-respect and esteem of your fellow-men, and have hopes of a better future?

Ah! my beloved brethren, let me give another turn to the question of my text: suppose you go on in this course of unbelief and impenitence? suppose you persevere in it against all the obstacles which a gracious God shall place in your way, and all His mercies and chastisements by which His goodness would lead you to repentance? suppose you live out this life as you have begun—*what then?*

What then, young man, when the hand of death suddenly arrests you, and you plead your youth, and He reminds you that it was foretold you, that "for all these thing He would bring you unto judgment?"

What then? ye guilty parents, when in characters of living fire you read these words—"suffer little children to come unto me, and forbid them not!" "bring up a child in the way he should go!"

What then? ye men of business, when in vain you plead the many occupations of your time, as you remember, how it was preached to you, almost to nausea, that "one thing was needful," and that you should "first seek the Kingdom of God and His righteousness."

What then? ye honorable men of the world, when before the last tribunal ye find you have no honour of God? *What then?* when ye shall see all, all fail of Heaven who have not been Christians on earth, who have not believed and repented here, and ascended on the wings of faith and love!

Oh! as you look over this life and all that it may offer you of its deceitful charms and its corrupting idols, think of death and of eternity, and ask yourselves—*what then!*

There is in modern Jerusalem, under the western wall of the temple, a place, the saddest place in all that sad part of the sacred city, the Jews' quarter; where every Friday the resident or stranger Jews resort: it is the wailing place of the Jews! There, with bowed head and often tearful voices, they bewail the desolation of their sanctuary and the affliction of their people! Oh, it must be sad indeed to see the children of Abraham kneeling there, in the sense of God's wrath hanging over them, with that deep and never dying love to Jerusalem in their hearts, and the honour of the temple their chief desire! See them, through all the long, long centuries of affliction, and eighteen hundred years of degradation and banishment, still cling to the truth of God's promises, and in the full belief of a coming Messiah, raise the tearful eye and cry "O Lord, how long!"

Brethren, is there not such a place of wailing in the life of every sinner? and often even in our churches? Are there not those in our congregations, who, not seeing the free salvation of God in Christ, and yet alarmed by the sense of their own unworthiness and condemnation, sit wailing and mourning? Oh, look up and take comfort, Messiah has come! He has come to *you*, and bids you look to Him and be saved! Arise, cease your unbelief, trust Him, and salvation is yours!

And oh, will there not be a wailing place for every impenitent sinner? an everlasting wailing place, where the lost soul in vain shall cry for a Messiah, aye more vainly than the wretched Israelite in Jerusalem? for to him the gospel still is preached.

May God save you from that wailing place, and give you faith and repentance!

The loving eye of Jesus is on you now, and in tender compassion He saith, "if thou didst know, even thou, at least in this day, the things that belong unto thy peace; alas, that they are hid from thine eyes!" God grant that the scales may fall from your eyes, that ye may believe and be saved! God forbid that it should be said of you, that they are forever hid from your eyes! Oh, no, no, no! My faith shall not yield and give you up; but as long as I have a voice to speak I will tell men of that love of God which bids them come, and pray Him to increase their faith! No, I never will give up my belief that His word is now as powerful as ever, to dispel every darkness. I never will give up my belief, that His love is as sustaining now as in days of yore. I never will give up any, as long as the message of Christ's love can reach them. May God incline your hearts to yield! You cannot say that these things are hid from you! Behold, the gospel banner is floating over you, and "free grace" is its motto! Behold, ye cannot attend this church without knowing that Christ came to save sinners, and stands and waits at the door of your hearts; that

God so loved the world as to give His only Son to die for it, and that

> The soul that to JESUS has fled for repose,
> He will not, He will not desert to his foes;
> That soul, tho' all hell shall endeavor to shake,
> He'll never, no never, no never forsake!

The Disciples were called Christians first in Antioch.
ACTS, xi. 26.

As a historical fact, this passage of the sacred narrative marks an epoch of the greatest importance. It records the second birthday of the Christian Church; the inauguration of St. Paul's work, who was commissioned to carry the Gospel from the narrow bounds of Palestine to the Gentiles, out of Judea into the world! In the very name *Christian* we recognize the hand of Paul. It set the young Church free from its Jewish bondage, and declared it to be the religion of the world, universal, catholic—"where there is neither Jew nor Greek; neither bond nor free, but all are in Christ Jesus." It gave a distinct form to the new religious element, and united all believers, irrespective of nationalities, under the sole name of Christ, and bound them together in that compact body which the world could not resist. From that moment the Church was emancipated from Jewish thraldom; from that moment she started to conquer the world.

In its practical bearings, the text is still more important. "The disciples were called Christians." That name which, though despised by the world, and hunted down by cruelty and persecution, soon became the greatest glory of those who believed in Jesus. Before the tribunals of the Roman magistrates, in the face of the infuriated mobs of the Jews, amidst the torments of their persecutors, and the flames of the stake, the universal shout of the faithful was: "I am a Christian!"

Can we say the same of ourselves? In the days of trials and persecutions men gloried in it; can we glory in it in the days of our prosperity, and when Christianity is a passport to respectability? *Here*, I say, are the practical bearings of the text upon ourselves. They were called Christians because they were distinguished from the world; the very name designated their coming out of the world into the Church.

Are *we* Christians, brothers?

It is truly astonishing that, with all the light which the Bible gives us, and which *we* may gather from the services and Collects of the Prayer-Book, embodying the known confessions of the most enlightened and advancing Christians of all ages and countries, that, with all this, there should be such a want of clearness and definiteness in most minds, to such a degree that it appears to many as "without form and void," and that the whole subject of *personal Christianity* assumes a mysteriousness, and is invested with a superstitious awe, as it were, which makes people shrink from the very contemplation of it, and which they know not how to consider in reference to themselves. And yet, brethren, the idea embraced in that glorious name, "a Christian," is something definite, tangible. All admit that there is a difference between Christians and those who are not; something which is peculiar to them as the children of God. What is it?

Of course it does not merely refer to outward profession, to outward church membership. The world is so ready to underrate these that we have to insist most strenuously upon their importance as "generally necessary" and incumbent on every true Christian; faith demands the confession of Christ in His ordinances. But, God forbid that we should ever present the name as the thing, the shadow as the substance. Nor does it mean an approval of the doctrines and practices of Christianity; for how often do we find a man's convictions and his practice at variance. Nor, finally, if, instead of taking the perverted notions and self-righteous conceptions of the natural man for our guide, we follow the teachings of the Scriptures, and the confessions and experience of intelligent professors, and the ripest Christians, does it mean that the Christian is one who pretends to be good and worthy of God's favour; who claims that name because he can boast of any attainments of his own, and stays his hope on any strength he possesses, any progress he can point to, the certainty that he has overcome every sin, the triumphs which *he* has obtained? Far from it, brethren! The very name indicates the reverse of this position: that in the sense of his own unworthiness, and knowing that there is no health in him, he does not plead *himself*, but Christ! relies not on his own right, but that of Christ; makes mention of nothing but Him and His merits. He owes all to Christ; and co fessing this, trusts in Him, and not in himself; he refuses to be called after himself, but after Christ. He professes not to be standing in his own strength and power, or rising by his own efforts and goodness, but to be one pardoned, saved, made righteous, and accepted in Christ, and sheer honesty compels him to confess this in his very name. He owes all to Christ, and owns himself as His. Purchased by His blood, rescued by His love, upheld by His grace, he does not owe his position and his hopes to himself, but to Christ; and therefore says, humbly, meekly indeed, in the sense of unworthiness and unprofitableness even in this character, and the feeble hold his faith has on him, yet all the more earnestly and anxiously and prayerfully: I am a Christian.

This is the great fundamental idea of his name. It does not exhaust it, for it has its farther bearings; but it is the true ground on which he stands. And it is this which makes the Gospel glad tidings to fallen man, and enables us to bring its invitation to all.

No goodness, no righteousness of our own, no attainments, no certain amount of strength, no security in our own steadfastness, can make us Christians; the very name *excludes* anything of our own. For *all*, we rest on *Christ*, and acknowledge it in the confession that we trust to Him and not to ourselves, and therefore are called *Christians*.

But it is true, this is only one aspect. Taking it as the starting point, the only ground on which we can stand as the children of God—we must carry out the idea embraced in it legitimately: We are *Christians*, *i. e.*, *Christ's*, and therefore must live as those who are *His;* our life must be by *His* power, will and law. *Ruled by Him*, and trusting in Him, we must do as *He* has done: *resist sin and live unto God*. Christ is not only our security from guilt and our plea before the Father, but also our *great and glorious example*, whom we must follow in our life; whom we must represent in our walk and conversation. We are Christians not only because we put our trust in Him for *justification*, but also for that grace in which we profess henceforth to endeavour to live as His soldiers and servants, enlisted in His warfare against sin, the world, and the devil; bound to His service in all holy and Godly obedience! This is the mind, with which we call ourselves after Christ, the high and holy calling we choose as those who are saved by Him!

And now we are prepared to say: who is a Christian? where do we find him, but in the man who, acknowledging his own unworthiness and helplessness, puts all his trust and confidence in Christ, and who, thus trusting his soul to Him, now strives to live the life of which Christ has given us the example, renounces sin, and lives to the glory of God in obedience to His holy will and commandments? And he is the *best* Christian who trusts *most in Christ* and *least in himself*, and counts his own attainments least; and, in the knowledge that he has not yet attained, neither is already perfect, strives most earnestly and constantly, by God's help, to live up more and more to the holy standard put up for us by Christ!

Now, if this is the true definition of a Christian, *what evidence can we have that we are such?*

Can we gather it from some such attainments, gifts and works, the impossibility of pointing to which keeps back so many; but which, as we have just seen, we renounce as giving us a *title* to this name? Why, that would be contradictory with our position! Or, can we go back into the past, and rest ourselves upon some sweet moment of assurance, some brilliant experience weeks or years ago, the absence of which distresses so many? My brethren, the evidences we need are *present* evidences; we must be Christ's *now*, or it will be of no avail to us that we fancied ourselves to be His years ago! We must be striving *now* to serve and obey Him; no past service can ensure us our position. For, at best, we are unprofitable servants, and never can lay up a claim or merit on which we could draw to comfort us in our present state! Whether we believed, repented, prayed, worshipped, worked five years ago, or a year ago, is nothing to the purpose unless we believe and pray and repent and work *now!* And if we never did so before, and do so *now*, we have all the evidence we need and can have, that we are Christians, Christians *now;* for no title is good except the present one!

People examine their faith, their repentance, their conversion, their prayers. That is all very well; and it is a sweet comfort to believe that God's grace has been with us; very encouraging to go on, and from the tokens of God's love in the past to continue to trust Him, to work on in hope! But to look to these as *our title*, as sources of comfort, and evidences of our eminent satisfactory Christianity? On the contrary, the true effect of self-examination will always be to humble us, to lead us anew to the foot of the cross, to seek for present help, to strive for greater attainments, greater evidences, to prove to us God's grace, manifesting itself in a life all aglow with the spirit of Christ. Why, brethren, it is not our *faith* which we pay as a *price* for our salvation! Salvation is free! The best we can say of our faith is, that it would be a miserable price; the best of us would have cause to doubt their character as Christians if it rested for its meritorious cause on strong and sufficient *faith*. "*Lord, increase our faith!*" is the cry of the sincere Christian; "*Lord, I believe; help thou mine unbelief!*" is the prayer with which we approach Him. That is no faith at all which makes a man satisfied with himself as a Christian, which makes him think he possesses a quality now which is his own. That, in fact, would rather separate us from Christ! Faith excludes all such boasting; it leads the soul out of itself to Christ; *all it has, all it glories in, is Christ!* That alone is saving faith, which *now*, at the present moment, and *forever* leads us anew to Christ, and *makes us cling to Him as if we had never had hold of Him before:* "Lord! save, or I perish!"

It is so with all Christian graces, with everything we hope for in Christ.

Take the highest point that can be made—and oh! that is made so superstitiously by many: *Conversion!* What—if you think you were converted years ago—what is that to you, unless you live as a converted person *now;* unless you *now* believe in Christ, *now* turn from sin, *now* turn to God in a holy, righteous and sober life? I should like to know what other proof of conversion we can have but this; and unless we have it now and henceforth, what use is it to us to believe that we had it in former days? "Turn us, good Lord, and so shall we be turned," is a Christian prayer. Do not wonder at the urgency with which we press this word "now," upon you. "Now is the accepted time," we must say to those who have never yet acknowledged Christ, and either fear that their day is passed, or vainly trust in a future season of repentance. "Now is the accepted time," we must say to those who have made a profession and humbly hope that the grace of God is with them. It is of no avail to have heard and obeyed once, if we are not now, "henceforth," as the Prayer-Book has it, walking in His holy commandments. "Grant, Oh! most merciful Father, for His sake, that we may *hereafter* live a godly, righteous and sober life, to the glory of Thy holy name!" The Christian's evidences always are *prospective*. But he who rests on his attainments, and grows careless because he has enough—brethren, he may fancy to have received but he has only deceived himself, and has no lot or part in His salvation.

Again: "Believe in the Lord Jesus Christ!" What does it mean but believe *now*—for *now* you need a Saviour, and need him *to the end!* Suppose a man had believed for twenty years, and he should now cease to believe. Whether such cases are actually possible or not, we need not discuss; we merely use it as an illustration. We must take people's faith upon their profession; that may be a false one, or they may have been mistaken: its *lasting* character, its *growing* nature, its *perseverance to the end*, alone can prove it *saving faith*. Suppose he should cease now to believe, *would he not be lost?* He is *now* without that Saviour, with whom faith alone connects him, *now* without that blood which alone cleanses him from sin, *now* without that righteousness which alone can shield him, and all his former faith could only heighten the heinousness of his present unbelief. And if we never had believed before—if we believe now, all our sins are pardoned, and we are accepted in

Christ. Oh, what comfort in that thought! What an appeal to all! It is a present faith we want, to bear us out in the present moment; we must have it now and ever or we are lost. And the only evidence that we are Christians, is that we believe *now!* The only evidence *when we die* that we are Christians, that we believe then! The only power to enter the gates of Heaven, that we can pronounce the *name of Christ.*

So with repentance: God's word saith "*repent*"— it is an ever *new*, ever present appeal. He is no Christian who does not repent *now.* "There is *now* no condemnation to them that are in Christ Jesus, who walk not after the flesh, but after the spirit"— *that is repentance!*

So with prayer! No reliance on some sweet moments of former intercourse. "Lord, teach us how to pray," for ever remains the true prayer of every God-aspiring soul.

So with works! No rest in what we *have* done! "Work out your own salvation" is the law for all Christians. "Strive to enter in," stay in, advance in, is the warning to every soul.

So with attainments! Not as though I had already attained, either were already perfect; but forgetting the things that are behind, I press towards the mark! "Only he that endureth to the end shall be blessed!" "Be thou faithful unto death, and I will give thee a crown of life!"

Ah! Brethren, here is the practical part, *man's part* of a final perserverance, which all can understand. Not that because we fancy ourselves once to have believed and been converted, that therefore we are elected and safe, no matter what lives we are leading now; but that, by the grace of God, *we hold on!* And only that title is good which, whenever we plead it, is verified by active, present faith, and love and obedience.

"The Disciples were called Christians first in Antioch." Antioch, the largest, but the most corrupt city of Asia; where wealth and power had their seat; where the world kept its carnival, and every luxury, and every licentious amusement of the degenerate Greeks of the East had their home; where all the frivolities and all the sins of a corrupt age, an unnatural civilization, and a luxurious climate were found together. Yet, *here* it was where the Gospel was to gain its first victories over the Heathen world, and the Church establish her power for centuries. Here the great apostle took the field, and from here he began his great missionary journeys, which eventually resulted in the triumph of Christianity over the world. Here was Satan's stronghold; here the world was in its fullest force, and ruled in its most attractive form; here the apostle attacked the adversary, and the pomps and vanities of the world, with its covetous desires; here sin reigned and slew its thousands; here the power of the Gospel brought salvation to its tens of thousands. God be thanked, *it is so still!* Christianity shows its power most gloriously where sin and the world and the devil seem strongest. In our largest cities, where the shadows fall darkest, the light of the Gospel is brightest! It was in Corinth that Christ assured the apostles that he had many souls. Oh, brethren, is it not so here? And can we not preach the Gospel boldly, must we not preach it faithfully here, amidst all the evil around us? Yes, and are we not encouraged to preach the Gospel to the most forlorn, the farthest gone, the least hopeful, the most hardened? Just as we must still and ever preach it to the best, the most experienced and promising. The *best* need the warnings and threatenings of God's word; the *worst* we invite to Him, whose blood cleanseth from all sin. To the most advanced we hold up their high and holy calling; to the most hardened we bring the promise of that power which quickens to a new and better life. To the foremost we say, "be not high-minded, but fear;" to the humbest we say, "despair not; arise, and wash away thy sins; call upon God; commit

THE NAME OF CHRISTIAN. 57

thyself to Jesus—He casts out none that come. Come thou with us and be a Christian!"

"The Disciples were called Christians first in Antioch." What has become of this first stronghold of the Gentile Church, this great Eastern metropolis? Earthquakes, fires, famine and the sword have laid it low; and the cross has fled before the crescent! Its splendid temples are crumbled in the dust, its lofty palaces fallen to the ground, its magnificent streets with their stately colonnades destroyed, its lovely groves and gardens desolated, its hundreds of thousands dwindled to barely six thousand inhabitants. Antakia, the modern Antioch, with its mud and straw houses, and miserable streets; with no Christian church, and fourteen insignificant mosques, is a living, but lingering proof that its candlestick has been removed, and its light quenched, because the living breath of Christianity died out! Oh, what a warning to us, the living, that no present prosperity, and no outward show of religion, no spiritual privileges and loud professions, no apostolic beginnings of a Church, are a security against the decay of true faith and earnest Christian life! And what a thought, that the absence of life and growth may be a judgment—"the candlestick removed"—and the sadness which fills us as we travel through the land

and see the evidences of weakness and decay, made sadder still by the fear, the possibility, that it is because the living breath died out: people fallen from their first love, and seeking first the things of earth and time, and not the kingdom of God, His truth and righteousness!

My brethren, what an appeal to us all, to avoid a similar retribution upon our country, our community, our congregations, ourselves—by making our Christianity more than a name, a *reality!* by coming out from the world—that heathen Antioch—and being separate unto the Church of the living God; by making our calling and election sure in a holy walk and conversation, and handing down to our children, and children's children, the mercies and blessings of the Gospel, the heritage of the Church!

Let us all remember, our course as Christians is still before us; we must grow in grace, or we cease to verify our character as the disciples of Christ; we must persevere *to the end*, or we falsify our Christian name, and are lost.

Oh, by all the warnings of God's word and God's providence, by all the sweet promises which He gives us, by all the tokens of His love and care and faithfulness; brethren, by all the issues involved and the glory to be revealed, by the love of your own selves, your children and your country, by the love of Jesus, which speaks to you so touchingly in the sacred emblem of His death and passion, we call you to a truly CHRISTIAN LIFE! Call for your faith, that it may grow stronger and stronger, and overcome the world; call for your *repentance*, that it may be deeper and more sincere, as you cry unto God, "make me a clean heart, Oh God, and renew a right spirit within me;" for your *prayers*, that they may be more fervent and constant to prevail with God. We call upon you to use every means of grace offered, and every power and faculty given you to glorify God; to strive to enter in at the straight gate, to walk worthy of your vocation, to approve yourselves in the sight of God and man. We call upon you to cultivate every Christian grace, the mind which was in Christ Jesus, the temper and moderation, the meekness, the purity and holiness of His life, the law-abiding patience and faithfulness in duty, the never-wearying, self-denying zeal and love which shall show what spirit you are of; and, in the sight of God, in your own consciences, in the sight of your enemies and before an opposing world, prove in your life and to your dying day that you are Christians!

Yes, my Christian brethren, my prayer to God is that you may so live that others, beholding your life and conversation, may know you as those who have "been with Jesus," and as they watch you, exclaim: "Behold a Christian!" May you so live, that when God shall send His holy angels to gather in His elect, and bring them to their blessed rest, to His kingdom and glory; they may read Christ's name upon your foreheads, and open to you the joys of Heaven; and that the hosts of the Church triumphant shall glorify God as they see you ascend and say:

Behold a Christian!

Man shall not live by bread alone, but by every word that proceedeth out of the mouth of God.

MATTHEW iv. 4.

The wilderness of Judea is before us, the mountainous tract which lies east of Jerusalem, and stretches along the plains of Jordan and the western shore of the Dead sea; a desolate region, bare and dreary, presenting everywhere yellow sand and grey rocks; scarce a tree to be seen; a few shrubs here and there on the slopes, and the intervening dells covered with arid grass, and some green bushes of cistus. In the days of Joshua, when the Israelites took possession of their promised heritage, six cities stood there, with their villages; but as the asphaltic lake buried the cities of the plain, so the wilderness encroached on the habitations of man; in course of time these cities disappeared, and the whole region between Jericho and the Dead sea became as stony and barren as it is now, deserted by man, and the haunt of wild beasts.

In this dreary solitude, a solitary wanderer is seen. From beyond Jordan, where, to fulfil all righteousness, He had been baptized, and where He was crowned as "the Son of God, in whom the Father was well pleased," He went as "the son of man,", "led by the Spirit," into the wilderness, to prepare for the great work of man's redemption. From the scene of glory He was transferred to the wilderness, and initiated in the ills and sufferings of human endurance. For forty days he stayed there, fasting and alone, bent under the scorching rays of a sun which, in unclouded lustre, hung in the heavens as in a brazen vault. Yet in that serene composure, in that calm countenance, in those blissful hours when his knee was bent by the desert shores of that sepulchral lake, or on the hard soil of the mountain-track, you could read, that—as in the last days of his painful pilgrimage on earth, with the death of infamy in the near prospect—so now, "though lonely He was not alone," for "the Father was with Him;" and though the earth withheld her food from Him, and His human nature felt the cravings of hunger, yet He learned the truth that "Man does not live by bread alone, but by every word that proceedeth out of the mouth of God."

Methinks I can see Him there!

From the scene of glory He was transferred to the days of trial and the scenes of temptation; and called to the combat with the adversary of God and man. He was alone. But ever and anon the communion with His Father in heaven, the solemn meditations of His soul were interrupted by a strange, unearthly influence. From the lake, over whose dreary, unrelieved flatness He cast His eye, and in whose sullen, sluggish waves He read the lessons of God's wrath, one would start up like a ghost from Sodom and Gomorrha, to whom the lusts of former days gave no rest under the heavy cover of his watery grave, and whisper in his ear terrible things of apostasy and human pleasure. As He stretched His weary limbs under the projecting rock and sought relief in the forgetfulness of sleep, one would lie down beside Him, and ply His sinless soul with images of forbidden joys, and the wish to leave the dregs of His bitter cup untasted, and cut short the day of trial and preparation. As He leaned exhausted against one of the few stunted trees, the same voice would reach his ear, and that weird eye, which put its spell upon Eve, look down on Him from its bending branches, and the wily tongue would bid Him cease His suffering, and, relying on His supernatural power, "command that these stones be made bread." About three miles from the road leading to Jericho, Mount Quarantania rises, fifteen hundred or two thousand feet in heighth, "distinguished for its sere and desolate aspect, even in this gloomy region of savage and dreary sights." Its highest summit now is crowned with a chapel, occasionally resorted to by the more devout pilgrims, while the eastern face, which overhangs the plain, and commands a noble view of the Arabian mountains, is much occupied with grottos and cells, the favorite abodes of pious anchorites. Here tradition fixes the spot of the Temptation. Here, as in the hour of His last trials, the Saviour said: "The cup which my Father hath given me, shall I not drink it? Is it not My meat to do the will of Him that sent Me, and to finish His work?" And as He turned the friend aside, and bade him "get behind Him," so now he bid the tempter flee, and said: "It is written, 'Man shall not live by bread alone, but by every word that proceedeth out of the mouth of God.'"

Brethren, let us turn from the wilderness of Judea to another and a greater wilderness—this earth; and from the Son of God to the pilgrim-truant of earth—to man, to ourselves, the children of a fallen race.

Ah, there was a time when this earth had not known the spoiler's touch, and when the seal of God's approval was set upon the work of His hand; when "the morning-stars sang together, and the sons of God shouted for joy," as they heard Him say that it was "very good." But a blight has fallen upon it, and the Paradise of earth has, by sin, been turned into a wilderness.

The Christian is no ultraist. He does not underrate the beauties which this earth bears, traces of the master-builder's skill. He does not scorn the work of man and the society of his fellow-pilgrims.

I have stood by the cataract as it leaped from the rock, and seen Niagara pour its ocean-wave into the abyss below, and in the deafening noise which rose from the mighty cauldron in which its waters roared and foamed, I heard the proclamation of God's power and glory; and in the rainbow-lustre which the sun or moon painted upon its everlasting spray, I read the promise of His mercy and peace. I have sped my gondola along the waters of Lake Como, and bathed my brow in the balmy atmosphere of the Italian sky; and as I gazed upon the picturesque shores, with their hills and valleys, and on that Southern beauty which is spread over all like a transparent veil, and saw the evening clouds curtain the heavens in deep folds of richest purple, fringed with gold by the rays of the setting sun, I felt as if I, too, could linger in this spot of idyllic beauty and dream myself upon the threshold of Eden. I have stood on the Alpine peak, the cloud beneath me climbing up the mountain side, and heard the booming of its artillery under my feet re-echoed in louder and louder peals from peak to peak, and saw the lightning, "like a bright, wild beast start from its thunder-lair," and when the veil was rent and the tempest gone, I looked upon a panorama in which grandeur and beauty embraced each other— the slope of the mountain covered with brilliant verdure, and dotted with picturesque cottages; the cattle feeding on the Alp, the dark range of fir trees, like a black belt lying round the shoulders of the mountain heights, towered over by the colossal head, veiled in eternal snow. I stood in the valley, the stream of molten snow rushing by my feet, bound by the freshest green; I leaned my face, flushed with excitement of the scenery, against the glacier's wall, all lost in the contemplation of such sublime beauty; and when darkness fell upon the valley, and the light of day had faded, as my eye was lifted to the distant peaks, I saw the rays of the sun, that had sunk behind them in the west, once more kiss their summit, and tinge their vigin veil of everlasting snow with the roseate hues of the Alpine glow; and I would veil my countenance, as Elijah wrapped his face in his mantle, when after the great and strong wind, and the earthquake and the fire, the Lord passed by him in a still, small voice.

Oh, God has made this earth very beautiful! And standing amidst the wonders of nature, my heart swells with adoration of the glory of God, and exults in the manifestations of His handiwork. On the wings of gratitude, who would not soar aloft and carol his matins of thanksgiving; or, in the sense of his all-embracing Fatherhood, when night draws on and the friendly stars look down upon him, welcome their softer beauty with the longing devotion of the vesper hymn?

I have looked upon man, and admired the achievements of the master-piece of creation. When I see him grasp the sceptre of this earth, and conquer the dominion of nature, search its secrets and command its forces, direct the course of the lightning and annihilate space, make his pathway in the great waters, and send his voice with the speed of thought from pole to pole, from the rivers to the ends of the earth, and perpetuate the impress of his mind and stamp his memory upon the face of this world to last as long as the everlasting hills, I rejoice in the truth, that God has "made him but a little lower than the angels."

I have revelled in the treasures of art and literature, and gazed upon the works of human genius till my imagination was filled with its productions, and I felt that there is that in man's mind which is akin to creative power, a token of his God-like origin.

I have shared the charms of society, and thankfully felt that it is good and pleasant for brethren to dwell together in unity; I have tasted the sweets of family life, and learned that, let this wilderness of earth be ever so dreary, let the waves of trouble roll ever so high, let life be ever so full of labour and sorrow, there is a green oasis in its desert waste—the sanctuary of Home, the peace of the fireside.

But still, brethren, with all the bright spots that smile on us from this earth, with all the innocent joys that are twined, like flowers, round the cup which this life hands to us, this earth *is* a wilderness, this life a scene of trial and suffering, and its cup has its bitter dregs.

It is a wilderness in the eye of that God who made it all glorious, but who, for sin, let fall on it the blight of His curse.

It is a wilderness in the eyes of the higher intelligences, that remember to have chanted the cradle-song of its primeval beauty, but who vainly seek that beauty now, for the smile of God no longer rests on it.

It is a wilderness, is it not, brethren, even in our own eyes? A wilderness and a life of trial and suffering. Who can deny that all the glories with which it is studded are but the fragments of the building, the broken columns of the temple that is shattered in pieces; that all the great and lofty traits in man, his mind and heart, are but faint traces of the image of God, in which he was created, but which was lost by sin? Aye, if we look beneath this outer crust of life, we find its hidden misery, and a skeleton in every house; we see decay at work and growing apace, until at the fiat of God it all becomes its prey. And if we shut out the sight of eternity, and the hope of Heaven, and look upon this earth alone—alas, it is a valley of darkness, watered by the tears of sorrow, the shadow of death brooding over it, with no star to give us light, no power to take away its fear!

And a wilderness, too, where the tempter draws nigh, and, "like a roaring lion, walketh about seeking whom he can devour." Under the luxuriant growth which hides the decay of time, and would lead us, in careless ignorance, to the banks of the sea of death, lurks poison! By the siren song of pleasure, or the glitter of gold, or the phantom of earthly fame, the traveler on the desert of this earth is made to linger in its oases and forget his home above; and, restless under the restraint of his probation time, *to command these stones to be made bread!* But happiness is not gained in this way, peace cannot be bought by sin, rest is not for the immoral pilgrim in the low-grounds of this fleeting existence. Yet happiness *is* his aim, the innate craving of his soul; and oh! if he could but command these stones to be made bread! If he could but satisfy his longing spirit! He may turn to the joys, or the treasures, or the honours of earth and seek relief, but as the roaming Arab rests only for a short time to refresh himself in the green pastures at the cooling spring of the oasis, he soon seeks something better and pursues his restless career. Adam dwelt in Eden, but the look of lust poisoned his bosom, and he thought he could not be happy without the taste of that forbidden fruit! And ever since has there been the longing for more than this earth can bring. Samson rose to glory, the honourable, God-befriended protector of Israel, but he looked for happiness beyond; alas, he vainly sought it in the voluptuous charms of the maid of Philistia! Solomon—his whole life was one pursuit of happiness; and a life of enjoyment and power such as few mortals ever tasted, brought, after its accompanying sins and idolatries, nought but the complaint of "vanity and vexation of spirit." Hazael looked upon the riches and power of Ben-Hadad and thought if he was King of Syria he would be happy; and in that crown he found a curse! The rich man in the Gospel hunted for happiness through all the avenues of earthly wealth and comfort, clothed in purple and fine linen, faring sumptuously every day. But he had to die, and awoke in hell!

Oh, brethren, these stones will not be bread! These barren wastes of earth afford no rest for the immortal spirit; its choicest summer fruits no food to stay the cravings of an infinite appetite!

But is there no rest? and no relief? and no joy and no bliss? no food to satisfy the hungry soul? no flood to quench its parching thirst? Thank God, there is! Rest for the weary and heavy laden, relief for all our sufferings, joy for the mournful, and bliss for the wretched. There is food which shall not fail—the heavenly manna in God's word; there is a well—whosoever drinketh of it shall never thirst again; there is a healing flood poured from Emmanuel's side; there is a gain—contentment and godliness, the riches which shall not see corruption; there is happiness—happiness in the love of God; there is peace—peace which the world has not given and that the world cannot take away; peace in the reconciliation with the Father, in the atonement of the Only Begotten! there is a wand *whose magic touch shall change these stones into bread—the religion of Christ!* "Man shall not live by bread alone, but by every word that proceedeth out of the mouth of God."

The word of truth, in which the believer's mind shall find rest in the search after the infinite.

The word of promise, which shall raise his soul from every depth of woe, in hope that maketh not ashamed.

The word of duty, which dries up the source of all his wretchedness, his sins; and opens the sluices of all happiness in the obedience of love!

This is the word which we bring you in the Gospel; this the bread and wine to which we invite your yearning souls, "without money and without price!" There is no happiness without it.

Follow me to that stately mansion which stands in yon lordly estate. Pass through its park and pleasure grounds, which betoken the wealth of the owner and cause many a beholder to sigh for such happiness; enter the lofty portals, crowned with the old family arms and see the men-servants and maid-servants, and the ornaments and conveniences which gold has here collected. Pass on through the spacious hall, tread lightly over those rich carpets, which seem to yield to the pressure of your foot; pass through those drawing-rooms, where splendour vies with taste; pass on,—and tread more softly—for I lead you to the dying couch of the wealthy owner. There he lies, his form emaciated, his eye sunk, his strength failing. There he lies, and around him are the tokens of his wealth and earthly happiness. What though the gold glitter in the purse which lies beside him—enough to purchase all the comforts of this earth; what though the richest curtains shade his bed of softest down; what though every wish and every want be supplied, and love, a mother's love, a wife's devotion, bend over the wasting form? Oh! unless Christ be in that death-chamber, Christ standing by that bed of suffering, these stones shall not be made bread: "Man shall not live by bread alone, but by every word that proceedeth out of the mouth of God."

Follow me to yonder alley, and wade through its filth and its atmosphere reeking with impurity, and go with me to that haunt of poverty, where every sight betokens want and suffering; rap against that tottering door which cannot keep out the chill and killing wind, and enter the room where the poor is dying. His bed mouldering straw; no comfort near, no human aid; his frame shaking under that racking cough, and humanity enduring its last extremities. And lo! in that uplifted eye, and those folded hands, those moving lips, that peaceful frame, you will see that if Christ be there, Christ to soothe and support, Christ with his blood to cleanse his soul from guilt and make it clean, Christ with His spirit to raise the soul to heaven and make it meet for the inheritance of the saints in light: though all that this earth can give be absent, and our death-bed as solitary as the hermit's cell, all these stones are made bread! "Man shall not live by bread alone, but by every word that proceedeth out of the mouth of God."

Oh, beloved brethren! ye who are still straying in the wilderness, still pursuing its earthly phantoms and its grovelling aims—but who cannot stay there long; for the death-bed must come, whether in affluence or in want, both to the good and the evil, the believer and the unbeliver—follow me now, when God calls to you so urgently, to Him who alone has the words of everlaslting life, who alone can change these stones to bread, and give you peace and rest. Follow me to Christ, and this wilderness shall blossom as the rose; streams of water shall burst out of the dry ground, and the tree of life be before you with healing in its leaves.

To the true Christian, that lives with God and abides with the Saviour, all around him becomes heavenly food, to strengthen and bless his soul; yea, every want of earth, and every pain and sorrow— channels that bear his ark into the haven of bliss. Religion turns the sands of the desert into gold, and its stones into the bread of heaven. That sun above him tells him of a nobler sun, the sun of righteousness, that has risen over him with healing in its wings; and though clouds may obscure it and darkness veil his horizon, behind that cloud he knows there watches a Father's eye, there beats a Father's heart, that yearns for his ransomed soul. The air he breathes, and the wind that fans his cheek, they are fraught with the promises and comforts and helps of God's Holy Spirit, by whose power he has been born again; which bloweth where it listeth, and sends his voice of love into his heart. "The earth with all its joys, the vault of heaven with all its wonders, the marvels and the beauties of created nature, the infant's cry, the wife's smile, the parent's grave, the bed of sickness, the voice of God's minister, the counsel of a friend, the reproof of an enemy, wrath and mercy, sorrow and joy, shame and hope, all thoughts, all passions, all delights, whatever stirs the mortal frame," all to him are vocal with God's Spirit, and tell him "to his great and endless comfort," that

"*Man shall not live by bread alone, but by every word that proceedeth out of the mouth of God.*"

In the day that thou eatest thereof, thou shalt surely die.

GENESIS ii. 17.

Man, as a creature, is subject to the supreme law of all creation: perfect obedience to the will of the Creator. As a moral agent, he is free to choose, and, at least as far as the exertion of his will goes, able to obey and disobey the laws of God. The apparent difference between the free will of the moral agent and the law of creature-obedience, which is without exception and imperatively binding, is harmonized in his *accountability*, by which his free will and choice is subordinated to God's law at the peril of his soul—the penalty of everlasting ruin.

But there are peculiar features in the nature and position of man which distinguish him from other moral agents. We know, in all, but three classes of these: First, there are those who have never fallen, but retained, and, no doubt, developed in greater perfection and blessedness, their original state of uprightness, having given themselves entirely to God and His service—these are the angels of God in Heaven. Then there are those who have irrevocably fallen, who have opposed their will and self to God in a manner unknown to us indeed, but which has thrust them forever out of God's sight, and confined to everlasting ruin—these are the devil and his angels in Hell. The third class occupies a middle ground, linked to both, and yet distinct from either. They are fallen indeed by disobedience and under the curse of God, banished from His sight; but they are not shut up in Hell, and not beyond the voice of mercy. Suspended between Heaven and Hell, as though it were in view of both, and destined either to the one or to the other sphere: they are placed upon this earth for a short span of time—but oh! one of infinite importance! a time of probation, of preparation either for Heaven or Hell. This is the position of man—a fallen moral agent, but with the invitation of the Gospel before him.

The difference is not in the terms offered; the same law of entire dedication to God has glorified the angels who obeyed, and damned the rebel spirits. The same law lies across the path of man. The difference is this: the choice is made, and made for all eternity in the case of angels and devils; the first dwell with God in everlasting light, the others are cast into outer darkness. But light and darkness alternate with man, for in his case the choice is still to be made. Indeed, it was made, and made for death, and laid us under the curse—but oh, the undeserved mercy of God! He offered us a second choice, and to make that second choice possible, took the blood of His Son in expiation of our sin! Oh, stand in awe, be humble, tremble all ye that are living under the blessings of this mercy: "For if God spared not the angels that sinned," but cast them down to Hell—to whom no second choice was given, but who are reserved in everlasting chains, under darkness, unto the judgment of the great day, because they kept not their first estate; for whom no Saviour died, and the Son of God became not incarnate (for verily He took not on Him the nature of angels, but He took on Him the seed of Abraham!): What condemnation can be great enough, what hell deep enough? for those who, after all these mercies, in spite of all this long-suffering and entreaty, notwithstanding all the humiliation, the suffering, the dying groan, the cruel death of God's own Son, notwithstanding all the strivings of the Holy Ghost and the constraining love of Jesus, again choose wrong; once more persist in their rebellion and deny the homage due to God, not only by right of creation, but, now, by right of redemption.

God created moral agents for high and holy purposes, and for a participation in His glory, which none but beings intelligent and of free volition could enjoy and were fit to bear. An eternity of glory and bliss was intended for them—the promised gift for their free acknowledgment of His power, wisdom and goodness, and their freely chosen resolution of devoting themselves to the lofty objects for which they were created. A test was necessary, where freedom of choice and separate volition were the peculiar features in the constitution of the subjects of these intended privileges and honours. How the loyalty of the angels was tested, we know not; we only know that the test was stood, and the surrender of self and every power made to God, by a sufficient number to fill the vast courts of Heaven with a holy and a blessed host. But that all others were by their failure disabled from ever serving God in holiness, excluded from His presence, and punished with His wrath.

But of the dealings with man, we have a full and authentic record. God had made him upright, created in His own likeness, and placed him on the new-created earth, resplendent with a beauty that had not known the spoiler's hand, and was untouched by the curse. He gave it to him for his portion, to rule over and subdue it and have dominion over every living thing, and gave him every herb and every tree. All her kingdoms were his tributaries, all her riches, her stores of wealth and comfort, all her attractions were for him. "All this," so God said in substance, "I give it with a liberal hand, a token of My love. Only be faithful to Me, and give Me thine heart!" But vain the love of God—the blessings which He showered down on man; vain the prospect of immortal life and glory, the threat of death with which He tried to guard His law and secure the loyalty of His creature. The test was but a trifle, one single forbidding command—"all else is thine! Be Mine; one tree in the middle of the garden—the tree of the knowledge of good and evil—thou shalt not eat of it. In the day that thou eatest thereof thou shalt surely die!" Ah! if Adam had but duly realized the existence of a holy God, and that He is a rewarder of those who diligently seek Him; if he had but had that general faith which is "the substance of things hoped for—the evidence of things not seen"—the great lever in every choice from motives; if he had had regard to the invisible future, and by faith apprehended its glory, and the reality of God's curse, and the infinite woe of banishment from Him who is the source of life and happiness, he could never have yielded to temptation! That one tree could not have become his all; the lust kindled in his heart could not have grown so gigantically as to hide from his sight God and Heaven, and immortality and glory, and to cover with its shadow the opening pit of destruction. But his lust overcame his faith and brought forth sin. He no sooner felt his power of disobeying God (which became clear to him only when a law was laid down,) than he worshipped Self and burnt the innocence of his soul as incense to his own gratification. He fell from God! He fell from God and under the sentence of death, which is the wages of sin! He fell from God! and with him fell his race, made in his likeness. "By one man sin entered into the world, and death by sin; and so death passed unto all men—for that all have sinned!"

The test had not been stood by Adam; Self had become his god; Heaven was lost! But oh, the depth of the riches, both of the wisdom and knowledge of God, and the inexhaustible fount of His love! Adam's next step would have been to pluck the fruit from the tree of Immortality, and thus have sealed his fate of deserved woe unalterably. Entering immortal life under the curse of his transgression, it must have clung to him through eternity, and forever exiled him and all his race from God. But thanks to God, and to His love to us in Jesus Christ: the expulsion from Eden prevented it. Death, the death of the body, was bidden to step in to suspend everlasting misery upon a new, but now ultimate trial. A short life of probation began for his descendants. In that life, the choice, and the same choice, is once more placed before us. We are wooed to obedience by the same promises, and promises of greater glory. We are warned off from every sin, as from the forbidden fruit, by the same threat: "In the day that thou eatest thereof, thou shalt surely die."

There stands in the garden-spot where the lines of each man's life have fallen, the tree by which he shall know good and evil. It bears the forbidden fruit, and God saith: "In the day that thou eatest thereof, thou shalt surely die!"

It is not every sin which proves the forbidden fruit, and the test of good and evil to every man. Each one has his own forbidden fruit; you have yours, and you yours, and I have mine. The same law of God is, indeed, the law of all; the same sins are forbidden to all, and the plucking of any one forbidden fruit brings death to the soul, unless Christ's blood is applied for its atonement, and its love overcome by repentance. But all men are not tempted by the same sins, each one has his own temptation, and if they yield to it their souls, they must surely die. The candid man will not be tempted to lie, but his forbidden fruit grows from another root; he may be overbearing in his treatment, and arrogant in his judgment of his brother-man. The liberal-handed benefactor of the poor may safely pass the tree whose fruit might tempt another to the sin of stealing; but his ambition may nurse the love of self and pride into enmity against God. The Ascetic will lend a deaf ear to the siren-song of revelry and forbidden joys, but he may cheat his neighbor in an over-reaching bargain. The naturally timid will not dip his hands in his brother's blood, but his forbidden fruit may be the sin of evil-speaking and slandering.

With all the multiplicity of sins, however, brethren, there are some great temptations, to one or the other of which nearly all are liable ; and well were it for us, if, whenever looking towards them, we could also read the label of God's own hand upon them—" forbidden fruit." Such are lust, pride, covetousness—the flesh, the world, and the devil.

Lust, which embraces both the grosser immoralities and the more dazzling vanities of the life of this world. It lies deep in the corrupt heart of man, and the open act is only the display of what has been the state of the person in secret. Here hangs your forbidden fruit, especially my youthful hearers, with passions wild and blood hot, and a mind yet undisciplined by the sterner duties and the sadder lessons of this life. The tempter may come to you gently and with a smile, and hide from your eyes the end to which his enticements lead; he will furnish you with specious pretexts, and lure you by the example of such as you would not think badly of. But the guile of the adversary is in all this, who is plying you with the same wiles by which he ruined Eve. He got her "to look at the tree," that it was " good for food and pleasant to the eyes, and a tree to be desired to make one wise," till she took of the fruit thereof and ate. Alas! how soon did she learn to know the good she had lost, and the evil she had chosen. Oh! flee, flee from the tempter and flee from the temptation, and hear God say, "in the day that thou eatest thereof, thou shalt surely die!" Look not at the red wine when it glows in the glass. The devil has more to do with the gross and beastly vice of intoxication than you may anticipate. Like all the sins of the flesh, it enslaves the whole man. It prepares the way for a multitude of sins, and links corruption with corruption; it casts a blight over all his actions and deprives him at last almost of physical ability to resist, ruins his respectability here, and finally drags him irresistibly down into the gulf of woe, which he saw yawn before him but could not avoid. Flee youthful lusts! abstain from vices with the names of which I cannot desecrate this house! There is nothing more dangerous in all your life than those things which feed the impure passions of carnal man. They are insidious as they are sweet; they gain upon you with gigantic strides and surround you as with invisible coils till you are caught and try too late to retrace your steps. Pass by the tree that tempts you to the forbidden fruit, lest its poison destroy the life of your soul! There are snares and dangers in the vanities and trifling amusements of the world; its fashion and its ways which have brought ruin to many a soul, which have eaten out every spark of vital religion from the professor who dared to tamper with such forbidden fruits; they have kept many a young person from adoring the Saviour, and led many a professor back into the world; *and their end was death!*

Pride, which makes a god of self, and thereby lowers us into slavery to the world and its ways; for it seeks distinction, honour among men, and flings aside the honour with God, because that rests only upon the humble and contrite heart. Pride, which genders unbelief and self-righteousness, which narrows the heart and never allows the soul to expand in wide-spread, generous love for our fellow-creatures! Numberless are the forms in which it is displayed, countless the deeds to which it may furnish the motive, and often what would be most lawful and acceptable and noble, becomes forbidden fruit, because of the touch of the hand of pride. It ogles the young, aspiring soul; it spreads, like the deadly Upas-tree, over the life of the man who feels his full powers and surveys his sphere of far-reaching influence; it separates the soul from God and Christ, and thus from life eternal. Like Lucifer, the proud man will be hurled from all his dreams of grandeur; a momentary meteor, he will shoot down into outer darkness, and learn too late that the day in which he feasted his soul with this forbidden fruit he doomed himself to death!

Covetousness! Of all sins the most insinuating, the most growing, which will strengthen with our days and be the portion of the soul that has outlived the temptation of all other sins, and tighten the grasp of the old man as he stoops toward the grave: it is the most hopeless, as it is the basest idolatry. You cannot serve God and mammon. Where your treasure is, there shall your heart be also. The love of gain and filthy lucre—alas, how many souls are burning on that altar; and souls that, perhaps, deceive themselves with hopes of heaven! If a man be a drunkard, an adulterer, or a liar; if he rob his neighbor, oppress the poor, or deal unjustly, he must give up his pretences to religion; the discipline of the Church, as well as the world, can reach him and cut him off. But a man may love his gold and at the same time keep his standing in the Church, and often only when he knocks at the gate of the Church in Heaven will he learn his doom—that Christ has never known him; he has plucked and glutted his soul with the forbidden fruit, and having left his riches this side of the grave, *eternity is one long and never-ending death!*

Oh, brethren! is it not true that for all of us there is found in this life a forbidden fruit? And how important the lesson we must learn *here to give it up, or we shall never see life.* How solemn to think of the import of this life of probation on earth! Heaven and hell meet here. Eternal happiness or eternal woe take their beginning in the souls of men here in this brief life on earth. We must forego the forbidden fruit that tempts the carnal mind, or we must die. If we pass from this earth without having gained this victory, we take with us no hope! All the power that is in Christ's atonement is of no avail to the soul that still feeds on the forbidden fruit. The love of Christ must have won our heart for Him, and made us strive against the love of sin, or the sentence of death follows us into the other world. Alas! for the momentary enjoyment of the forbidden fruit, to cast away eternal life and the loving kindness of God, which is its highest glory!

Oh, brethren! how soon may death arrest our career on earth? The graves are yet fresh in our midst, where we have deposited the remains of many who were dear to us as dear can be, and many of whom were cut off in the flush of youth and by a sudden visitation. Have you never known God's sore punishments to pass through the land? The pestilence that, with its poisoned scythe, mows down the young and the old. The war which has bleached our fields with bones and swept off its thousands into an untimely grave, which we still decorate in memory of our dead? The wind that has often come to us across the watery waste with a mournful sound, bearing to our trembling hearts the last notes of the requiem it sung over multitudes, multitudes that now sleep at the bottom of the sea? The famine that but now has sent its starvation-cry across the ocean from a sister-isle? Believe me, beloved brethren, whatever the tragedy be which sends the shuddering thrill through the land—railroad wrecks, sunken ships, fields of blood, the poisonous pestilence, the devouring flame, or the hollow-cheeked famine—not one soul fell a victim to their fatal power but he carried with him his check upon the other world, "a draft upon heaven or draft upon hell, payable one moment after death," and by the love of the forbidden fruit or the love of Christ, all have been judged of God.

Men look with horror upon Adam's sin. They cannot understand how he could pluck that fruit when God had said, "In the day that thou eatest thereof, thou shalt surely die." But in that ye judge him, ye condemn yourselves! Every one who does not forsake his sins and trust in Jesus, would have acted just like him or worse—*is* acting, brethren, worse than he. 'Tis true, Adam was uncorrupt before the fall, but in the Gospel we offer you a healing balm for that corruption. The motives for giving up your sins and turning to God, and dedicating yourselves to His will and service, are now infinitely greater than they were for him. God was his Creator, but He is your Redeemer! *The blood of all his children may be upon* HIS *head, but on* YOURS *is* THE BLOOD OF CHRIST!

Tekel—thou art weighed in the balances, and art found wanting.

DANIEL v. 27.

The grandeur of the ancient world is passed away. But its traces are left on the surface of the earth, and its influence is perpetuated in the civilization of our day.

The traveler on the Nile beholds the narrow valley studded with the monuments of her former glory—the pyramid, the obelisk and the sphinx; and in her mountain sides still stand the tombs which, in their beds of rock, embrace the embalmed generations of the men that lived millenniums ago. — Jerusalem, which was visited with a destruction, the like of which is not recorded in the annals of history, still lures the pious pilgrim to her sacred mount. — Athens, amidst her broken pillars, her ruined temples and her mutilated statues, struggles into a new civilization, as the withered tree will often clothe its naked branches with a second growth of verdure. — Rome, which oftener than any other city saw the conqueror within her walls, and was sacked and burned repeatedly by the ancient and the modern barbarian, still proudly rears her throne upon the seven hills. Ancient Rome still lives in her laws, which form the nucleus of all our codes of law; and modern Rome shouts "*vivas*" to the new king that has once more united Italy under her sway; and papal Rome wields her sceptre over more souls than ever bowed to the power of her Cæsars.

But *Babylon the great is fallen and is no more!* She has left no "footprints on the sands of time." Posterity owes her nothing but *the lesson of retributive justice* upon the wickedness of man. *The plains of Shinar are a desolation!*

As the traveler approaches it from the East, on the road from Bagdad, and stands upon the earthen ramparts which tradition and historical speculation assume to be the most northern remains of the ancient city, there spreads before him a boundless plain. The Euphrates, with its dark belt of evergreen palms, which flowed through the middle of the vast metropolis, still rolls its flood along; but it winds through a naked and hideous waste. The foot of man does not rest there, the hand of man does not build there. Where once stood the city that covered more than the area of London, replete with palaces and gardens, and filled with riches such as now fill only the dreams of fiction; where smiled a country that gave her harvests almost without labour and bloomed as a garden, dissected with the numerous canals, which sent the fertilizing waters of her glorious river into all its parts; where was the mart of the world, and roads of traffic centred, that combined the trade of the North and the East and the West; where was the meeting-place of caravans, and where ships enlivened the harbour, that came laden with the gold and choicest spices of the coasts of Persia and Hindostan: *there now all is one great wilderness and solitude;* "owls start from the scanty thickets and the foul jackal skulks through her furrows." Truly, "the glory of kingdoms and the beauty of the Chaldeans' excellency is as when God overthrew Sodom and Gomorrah. Wild beasts of the desert lie there, and their houses are full of doleful creatures; and the wild beasts of the islands cry in their desolate houses, and the dragons in their pleasant places, *for her day is come.*"

But the text brings us back to the days when Babylon was yet standing, and glorying in all her beauty and wealth, "the Lady of Kingdoms." "Is not this the great Babylon that I have builded?"

Only a few decenniums had passed since Nebuchadnezzar raised her to the pinnacle of glory and made her the mistress of nations. Judea fell before her, and Jerusalem sent her captive sons to the rivers of Babylon. Egypt was defeated by her proud warriors, and Phenicia crouched under her yoke. Like a new city, old Babylon rose from her former position under the ambitious monarch and his queen. The temple of Belus was finished; the new palace erected, whose circuit was equal to that of a moderate-sized city; and the gallant king, to please his Median queen, recalled her mountain scenery, in the verdant terraces which rose four hundred feet above the ground, the wonder of the world. The spoil of vanquished countries loaded her treasury; her commerce gathered the finest wools and shawls from Cashmere; emeralds, jaspers and other precious stones from Bactra; gold and gold dust from the Indies; and extended through Phenician traders and the ships of Tarshish down the western coast of India, and brought from the island of Ceylon the rarest spices and choicest pearls. Mechanical arts and mathematical science, astronomy and astrology, the art of working in metal, and her woolen manufactures, which wove those splendid Babylonian robes (so far famed for delicacy of texture and brilliancy of colour): all presented a state of civilization which the East had not seen before. But, alas! she bore within her the curse of luxury and effeminacy. Her very religion—the religion of Belus and Mylitta—only ministered to the grossest passions of the human heart. The effeminacy and licentiousness of her inhabitants beggars description, but makes it plain how a few years could lay the proud city in the dust.

Times had changed since the death of the great king. Her power sank, whilst her luxury and oppression continued. And her lofty walls and brazen gates were but a poor safeguard against the new foe, that brought his hardy soldiers before them. *In her security she fell; in the midst of revelry, her doom overtook her!*

It was a festive day in Babylon. "Belshazzar, the king, made a feast to a thousand of her lords."

Up the broad flight of steps, guarded right and left by colossal statues of crouching lions, the guests hurry towards the grand portal, a magnificent gateway, formed by the towering statues of winged bulls with human faces and crowned with the royal tiara. The first entrance led to others of a similar construction, until the great hall is reached where the feast is spread on tables of gold and silver, and ivory and costly wood, with cups most curiously carved or covered with inscriptions. The tiles they tread on are filled with the records of the kingdom; and on the walls, where the bricks are covered with plaster, and the richest colours—tastily distributed—divide and frame the paintings, their country's glory is represented in triumphal marches, and trains of captives suing for pardon, or tributaries bringing gifts. The hall itself stretches along to an immense length, and at the end is the great platform, where, in distant magnificence, reposes the king "to drink wine before his lords." The whole is lighted with lamps and chandeliers. The lighted hall and the illuminated gardens call the people to the courts of the palace, and spread the feast from the lords through the masses of the frivolous inhabitants.

And now the music animates the festive assembly, and the wine glows in the glass, and the passion is fired, and the drunken shouts are heard; and the dancers rise—the women whom Babylonian custom admitted to their feasts; who, having long laid aside their modesty, now free themselves of the encumbrance of the flowing robe, and madden the excited senses of the luxurious king and lords by their attractive art.

Behold a Babylonian Bacchanal! What though the Mede and Persian lie before the city: the high walls of Babylon shall laugh at them! What though prophecies have rung in the ears of the revelers: their gods, their gods that speak to them from the sculptured walls, and point them to the painted triumphs and the prosperity and days of mirth and revelry their favour had bestowed upon them, their gods of gold and silver and brass shall overrule the predictions and the threatenings of that stern Jehovah!

"Bring hither the golden and the silver vessels from Jehovah's temple, and let Babylonia's king and princes, their wives and concubines, offer them in festive glee to Babylonia's gods!"

And the golden vessels that were taken out of the temple of the house of God, which was at Jerusalem, were brought, and the king and his princes, his wives and his concubines, drank in them. And the shouts rose higher, and the laughter grew wilder, and blasphemies and obscenities mingled with their mirth, as they drank wine and praised the gods of gold and of silver, of brass and of iron, of wood and of stone.

Ah! brethren, how many a Babylonian Bacchanal is witnessed on this earth! "The harp and the viol, the tabret and pipe and wine are in their feasts; but they regard not the work of the Lord, neither consider the operation of His hand." How many lives are nothing but a Babylonian Bacchanal, "God being not in all their thoughts!" Yes, brethren, many a Belshazzar's feast is met with, with its wild devotion to the glee of earth and the mad excitement of the fleeting moment; whilst around the thoughtless revelers, as the Medes and Persians around the walls of Babylon, are the armies of the avenging angels of God's justice!

But hark! What means this sudden, piercing cry? and now—the dead silence which succeeds the noise and laughter? What means this sudden change? Behold the king, how he starts! and his royal mitre falls from his head, and his hair seems to stand on end; his eyes roll wildly, and ever turn to that bright wall, lighted by the chandelier! And his color has changed "and he begins to tremble;" the joints of his limbs are loosed, and his knees smite one against another. See the pallor that spreads over all faces, and the trembling lip and staring eye—staring on that bright wall, lighted by the chandelier!

"In that same hour came forth fingers as of a man's hand, and wrote over against the chandelier upon the plaster of the wall of the king's palace."

Oh king! in vain dost thou appeal to the wisdom of thy astrologers, thy Chaldeans and soothsayers—*it is a message from God unto thee!* and none but His prophet shall read that writing.

There stands the young prophet, the despised son of the despised captives of Judea, who, disdaining the king's gifts, his scarlet robe and golden necklace and high office, boldly read his doom: "*Tekel—thou art weighed in the balances and art found wanting!*"

In that night Belshazzar, the king of the Chaldeans, was slain. In that night the strong walls and brazen gates of Babylon ceased their protection; the faithful river ceased its service. According to prophecy it was turned into another channel, and the army of the Medes and Persians walked through its dry bed into the city and surprised the drunken revelers. *In that night Babylon fell;* Darius, the Median, took the kingdom, and "*Belshazzar, the king, was slain.*"

Brethren, have you ever had thoughts of such a night? Ever had forebodings of such a night? Have you ever known persons who had been contented to live "without God" in the world, when they saw the handwriting of death, send for the minister, the prophet of God, to smooth their dying pillow? And ever doubted the probability of a peaceful death after a wicked life? Ever feared that the awful word "*wanting*" should be uttered over the soul that had begun to think of God and repentance *only when life was over?* Have you not, in that dread moment, understood the poet's description—

>How the frantic soul
>Raves round the walls of her clay-tenement,
>Runs to each avenue and shrieks for help,
>But shrieks in vain!

There is a painting of solemn import found in the Campo Santo of Pisa, "The Triumph of Death," by Andrea Orgagna. It dates from the second half of the fourteenth century, and is *an affecting representation of the triumph of death over all the splendour and grandeur of earth and worldliness.* To the right of this large painting is a group of men and women, engaged in music and conversation. The flowers with which the ground is covered, the arbour of the myrtle and the orange in which they are gathered, as well as the amorettes that hover round them, are all intended to paint the soft, luxurious life of earthly pleasure and the sweets of love. But, unperceived by them, there hovers close to that idyllic arbour the *messenger of death*, with wings full of eyes and the scythe lifted for action; this is *death unexpected!* — To the left a noble hunting party—king and queen, and knights and squires and dames on prancing steeds, with falcons on their glove and the hounds following. But suddenly the horses start and turn; before them lie *three open coffins—they are riding into mouldering dust.* This is the *warning of death.* — In the middle of the painting *death is at work;* and king or queen, noble or low, bishop or priest, are lying on the ground, their souls escaping with their last breath in the shape of little babes, and the angels, good or bad, waiting to receive their own, and carrying these to the mansions of heaven, or hurling those into devouring flames.

Now, my beloved brethren, are you of those whom death shall surprise unprepared? or who will take his warning *now* while time is yet given you? He comes, He surely comes to all of us, and stretches us low in the indiscriminate summons he gives to the good and to the evil. "Oh! wicked man, thou shalt surely die!" is said to all. Is it not probable that the words of the prophet, "This year thou shalt die," are said to some of us? And is it not absolutely certain that the day will come, when God shall say to him that is only thinking of heaping up treasures and guarding earthly riches, or to him that forgets eternity in the pursuit of passing pleasures and earthly fame: "Thou fool, this night thy soul shall be required of thee."

Oh! if we could but see the invisible hand which now is writing our doom upon these walls; if we could ascend and see the balance that is held in the hand of the Judge who judgeth righteously, and take warning, *all* take warning, *ere it is too late*, and ere the sentence "wanting" is irrevocably pronounced.

Let the eye of faith transport us, brethren, from the hall of Belshazzar and that awful handwriting.

to the hall above and to the real balance. Behold how the whole race of Adam, in the long line in which it has traveled for six thousand years over this earth, stands there, and *all are weighed, weighed in the balances!*

Behold! they come from the fireside, they come from the tented field; they come from the hermit's secluded cell, they come from the public mart. They start from the bed of luxury, they start with the sweat on their brow. They are summoned in youth, they are called in old age; from the workshop, the ball-room, the study, the bench—they must follow the merciless call. The promising youth, the hopeful aspirant, the loving mother, the only son—death summons all. The good and the bad, those prepared and those unprepared—all must come. The miser is called away from his gold, the drunkard from his cups, the laborer from his honest work, the pious from their prayers, the king from his throne, the prisoner from his dungeon, the rich or the poor, the happy or the unhappy—*all, all* are found in that long procession, and *all are weighed in the balances.*

Those balances! They are held in the hands of Eternal Justice, and the book of God's law lies in one scale. *Come on ye children of men and fill the other scale; ye must be weighed!*

There comes the murderer, the thief, the drunkard, the adulterer and slanderer; and fain they would turn from that dread balance, for with blanching cheeks and trembling lips they confess that they bring nought to God but crimes.

There goes the miser with his gold, but ere he reaches the balance it has crumbled into dust.

There go the great of the earth with their glory, but it is dissolved in air ere they can be weighed.

There come those whose only pursuit on earth was pleasure, and behold it is turned to remorse; who lived in lust and revelry, and scorpions scourge their souls.

Here goes the man of learning, the student of this world's philosophy. Ah! as he approaches that balance he sighs that he forgot to seek *that wisdom which is from above, which makes wise unto salvation.*

There comes *the moral and the upright man of the world*, that has been honest and dealt fairly and lived decently; but oh! as he looks upon that law and sees its terrible character of holiness revealed, he dares not throw his morality in the scale, he stands convicted: *Wanting!*

Lo! there goes one, and the clamour of the multitude follows him, whom he hath fed and warmed; he has been generous and benevolent, and given his goods to feed the poor. There goes one that gave his body to be burned, and his good and glorious deeds are thrown into the scale—*wanting!*

But *make room!* There comes the *Christain professer*, and boldly lays his profession of religion in the vacant scale. *Depart! empty professer, thou art found wanting!*

Again one comes and lays his prayers there—*wanting!*

Or lays his tears of penitence into the balance—*wanting!*

Or puts his good intentions there—*wanting!*

His pious aspirations—*wanting!*

His sincerity and struggles—*wanting!*

Ah! brethren, learn—learn while time is given you, that nothing you can bring of your own *can* turn the scales and save you from the sentence "*wanting!*" And that none, and not the best of your good works, can meet the claims of the law of God and balance the scales!

Behold! there comes one, with his eyes cast down and with the sense of utter nothingness in his heart; that brings no ransom in his hand and pleads no action of his own. He comes with the confession of unworthiness, the acknowledgment of his just condemnation. He comes, and all-despairing of himself he *dips his hand into the stream that flows from Jesus' side, and lays His blood, the blood that bought him, in the scale*—: and the scene is changed! the law is outweighed! The blood of Jesus, and that blood alone, has met its claims, has borne its curse and blotted out its handwriting; and the angels of heaven receive the wayfaring traveler, who stands before God in the name of Christ, and the eternal mansions ring with the shout of victory—

"Thanks, thanks be unto God, that giveth us the victory through our Lord Jesus Christ!"

The times of this ignorance God winked at, but now commandeth all men, everywhere, to repent.

Acts xvii. 30.

Paul at Athens—the city whose name calls up all that is great and attractive in this world's wisdom. On the foundation of her ancestral glory she rose like a Pharos of the ancient world, where was culminating all its light of literature, art, science, philosophy; and like the gilded spear-head of her protecting goddess on the Acropolis, that could be seen flashing in the sun from the far-off sea, shed its beams far and near, and brought every country and nation within the circle of her attractive power.

Paul on Mars' Hill! where, from time immemorial, the most august court of judicature had sat to pass sentence on the greatest criminals, and to decide the most solemn questions connected with Religion. There Paul had been arrested while discussing with the loquacious and inquisitive Athenians the things pertaining to God, and was carried up by his accusers to confront the awful tribunal, on whose decision hung life and death, *as a setter-forth of strange gods.*

Above him the canopy of heaven, around him

the plains and mountains of Attica, and in the distance the expanse of the Ægean sea. Immediately before him the Acropolis with the glorious Parthenon and the colossal statue of Minerva, and a thousand other images, many of them glittering with silver. And as his eye ranged from temple to temple which met his view wherever he turned, his spirit was stirred within him to denounce the superstition which thought that "the Godhead dwelt in temples made with hands." And as he glanced over the images and statues of their deities, which crowded the city in such numbers, that one of their satirists declared it was easier to find a God in Athens than a man; almost under the shadow of the bronze colossus of its champion goddess, towering from its pedestal on the rock of the citadel, he boldly proclaimed that the Deity "was not likened to gold, silver, or stone graven by art and man's device." *The poor and solitary Hebrew* met the assembled wisdom and power of the most civilized community of the world, and not in enticing words of man's wisdom, but in demonstration of spirit and of power, he revealed to them " *the unknown God*," he preached to them *Jesus and the Resurrection*, and pointing to the risen Saviour, who should come again to judge the world, called them to the faith of the Gospel—"the times of this ignorance

God winked at, but now commandeth all men, everywhere, to repent.

The times of this ignorance! And what times, brethren, did the Apostle designate with this sweeping declaration! I look through the book of history and find no brighter page; I take the map of this globe and pass from land to land, but there is no spot so glorious by the achievements of the human mind, so luminous with the glow of civilization, as the city of Minerva. The times of her growth and development were the times when genius winged its flight over the earth and liberty broke the chains of despotism, when beauty first dawned upon the conception of the human mind, and poesy and thought became new powers in the life of man. Ah! they were the times when a line of heroes, sages and statemen passed over the stage of life, who still are the watchwords of our youthful enthusiasm and the lofty standards of our riper years; which produced the leading types in all that men call great—Solon the legislator, Pericles the statesman, Demosthenes the orator. The times when philosopy and science left the dreamy cradle of the east and built the lofty fabric of human knowledge, when Socrates taught ethics and Plato his idealism; when Aristotle lived and contributed more to the stores of human knowledge and exerted a greater influence upon the human mind, and gave a more lasting direction to its progress (lasting to this day) than any other uninspired man on earth! The times which were peopled with poets and writers and artists in painting and sculpture, who still are the standard of beauty and perfection, and whose works still refine our minds and beautify our lives and adorn our houses; the times, in short, when lived the men, the light of whose genius and power has not been quenched by the lapse of long, long centuries; at whose feet we still are sitting to learn the first and often the highest lessons in politics and science and literature and art, and without whose inexhaustible legacy this world would be deprived of many of the highest possessions of humanity. *These* are the times, beloved, which the Apostle boldly calls the *times of ignorance;* not the times of hyperborean darkness, not the night of barbarism and cannibalism—the times of the highest human development and civilization then known, and the premise of the glories of our present culture! *And yet, times of ignorance!* for what are all the gains of human wisdom without the knowledge of God—His holy law and His redeeming love?

Here, at the very threshold of the Church, its herald threw down the gauntlet to the greatness and the wisdom of the world; and from the high platform of revealed truth—the truth as it is in Jesus, the truth which alone declares the origin and condition, the purposes and ends, the eternal relations and necessities of man—beholds the subordinate value of everything else, and sees darkness settle over the scene which is only lighted by human wisdom, without the knowledge and the faith and obedience of the truth of God, the one thing needful for His creatures in time or in eternity.

And eighteen hundred years, my brethren, have not changed the issues. Let us take this nineteenth century. Ah! it is not necessary for me to carry you along the oft-trodden road of its praise and glorification, and give a rapturous description of its blessings and privileges or gains and triumphs. The advances we have made in every department of human greatness, in knowledge, science, literature and art, in politics, commerce and social philosphy, in deep searchings and lofty speculations: they are the theme of a thousand orators of the day, who find no more fertile or more pleasing topic than to congratulate the world upon its greatness and flatter it with the excellency of its civilization. And ours *is* a glorious time with all its trials, crimes and humiliating experience. Our culture bears richer fruit than any other. The germs of the former days and civilization have developed in an abundant harvest, and the new element of Christianity has called forth forces and new ideas, and roused up capacities, which have placed us in every respect ahead of the palmiest days of antiquity. The powers of nature are at our command as they were never before; experience has taught us its lessons, society contains new sources of power, new means of advancement; and a momentum has been given to our times that makes us reach results at a bound, which by-gone generations groped after in tedious and circuitous routes. The whole world is waked up and alive to every important measure and question. Monopolies have ceased, and every part of this globe contributes its due to the work of our race and the promotion of our civilization. And yet— after admitting everything that can be claimed; what is our life and what are our gains, and what is our civilization worth, if the truth of God is not its life and its light? What does all our glory amount to if it lacks the true glory of man—*godliness*?

The festive hall, brilliant in the glare of countless lights, and adorned with all that taste and genius can suggest: it is very beautiful and very dazzling, and many a pleasant hour may be lounged away in its blaze. But blot out that sun which lights the heavens and the earth, and will your lighted hall replace a darkened world? Just so when the light of truth is hid, and when the love of God does not rule—what can you give us but darkness and misery? When God is not in all our thoughts, when His word is not the light by which we walk, His righteousness not the first and paramount element in our life—" What shall it profit a man if he gain the whole world and lose his own soul?" Ah! this truth is of infinite importance, and reaches into every department of our private and public life. We may study the laws of nature, but it will be worse than wasted time if we do not find and worship in them the *God* of nature. We may multiply inventions and comforts, lay out new lines of communication by land and by water, but cannot lay out a new road to *heaven!* You may thunder your speeches in the Capitol and your rostra may resound with eloquence unparalleled; you may call your great political meetings and consider the dearest interests of your country; the patriot's fire may animate your tongues and your hearts, and your greatest energies be roused; but, I tell you, if the knowledge and love of God are not the paramount element in your counsels, if in all you attempt, you do not place your duty to God *first*, if in all your works you do not serve God and His Christ—the light which is in you is darkness and all your wisdom turned to ignorance! God forbid that we should speak slightingly of patriotism, of the duties to our country and any legitimate employment, the daily work God has appointed us on earth. God forbid that we should not value our privileges and gratefully rejoice in the blessings with which our earthly life is crowned. But, brethren, *God first*, and then the world! and the world *only* in accordance with God's laws and will! Ah! it is true as the Gospel itself, that no country and no community, and no house and no individual can be blessed, unless we seek first the kingdom of God and His righteousness, unless we believe and live and act as Christians. And knowing how constantly men separate their interests and their work in the world from the thought of God; how many live and make their plans and pursue their ends "without God" and "without Christ;" how many there are to whom God still is "an unknown God" and Christ "an unknown Saviour," I address the words of St. Paul to all: "The times of this ignorance God winked at; but now commandeth all men, everywhere, to repent."

The times of this ignorance God winked at!

Here, beloved, is a glimpse into the mysteries of God's mercy, clear enough to quiet the mind when speculating on the condition of those who lived before the Christian revelation, or whom it has not yet reached. But this is apart from my theme. The question for *us* is this: Are ours the times of ignorance which God will wink at—that is, overlook, bear with? And who is there here who could affirm or believe this? Ignorance, indeed, is fallen to many, but is it excusable or not? Is it by necessity or wilful? and if wilful, does it not bring us into condemnation? And if so, oh, what else can we preach you, but repent! repent! for you are without excuse?

The Gospel has risen upon the world, and from the rising to the setting sun its glad tidings and its solemn calls are proclaimed. And if there be on this globe some darkened spots, where Salvation through Christ has not yet been preached: the world which *we* know, the world in which *we* live, is all in a blaze with the light of truth shed on it, the Salvation of God offered it. Here, in this country, more favoured in religious things than perhaps any other, the Gospel is known to all; here, in this house of God, known to every soul, and if it is hid, it is hid only in its saving power. "If our Gospel is hid," said the Apostle, "it is hid to them that are lost!" Oh, gracious God! shall it be so with any of you? Brethren, you can plead no other ignorance but impenitence. Many have been the times, when God placed Himself in your way, and reasoned with you of temperance, righteousness and a judgment to come! when He knocked at the door of your heart, to bless you with His truth and presence!— You may live immersed in your business and bury all other thoughts in the cares of your earthly pursuits. But has the time never been, when the thought rose in your heart that this was not all, nor the best thing of this life, and that there are higher riches to be gained, and that there is a lasting portion for the soul? God then tore away the veil of ignorance and spoke to your soul: *you are without excuse!* — You may follow the gaieties of life, and pass from pleasure to pleasure, and where is there time for searching into the truth! And yet you have had the moment of satiety and weariness, and perhaps remorse; and longed for something better than the husks of a frivolous world. God had lifted the curtain from the sanctuary of truth, and you cast a longing look within; your ignorance is gone—*you are without excuse!* You may be the slave of lusts and vices, and your tastes be only earthly, but there have been days and weeks perhaps, when "a fearful sound was in your ears." Of all men in the world, *you* are those who most frequently and loudly have heard Him call to you: repent! You had no innocence to lose, but you have lost your ignorance—*you are without excuse!* Ah! there is no life which has not had its lessons, where, either in the day of rejoicing or in the day of sorrow, the thought of God and His Salvation has not obtruded; and oh, that souls still are ignorant of the way of life, who perhaps have seen the heavens opened as a little babe was borne aloft, or a beloved parent or friend seen to ascend on the wings of faith and love; and can you forget the truth of eternal life, and refuse to repent?

My brethren, what can we do, what can I say to rouse you and prevail? Shall I bring up the charge of sin?—your heart trembles at it now! Shall I call up the terrors of God's vengeance?—will fear drive you into the love of God? Shall I rehearse again the plan of Salvation, pressed home to you a thousand times, and yet a thousand times in vain? Shall I open again the riches of Christ's grace, and the freeness of His invitation, and bid you come, with all your sins, "just as you are?" Oh brethren; but you must come with the prayer and the resolution to be made better, made holy and like Christ; this is the repentance demanded; and without that holiness, which results from it, no man can see the Lord! *I* have no power, no strength, no wisdom, to persuade hearts that have resisted so often and so long. *Thou gracious Saviour, and Thy constraining love alone*, can win the heart and bring it to repentance. Oh, think of Him, beloved, the Only Begotten Son of God, who became obedient unto death, even the death of the cross—and why? to pay the penalty for our sins and make a way for us to God and Heaven? surely! but also to conquer with His bleeding love the proud heart of apostate man, and excite in it a feeling of love to that God who loved us and gave His Son to die for us!

Fellow-sinner! does not your heart thrill at the sound of those names: Gethsemane and Calvary? The Son of God, sinking under the weight—oh that weight!—of the sins of the whole world that was laid upon Him; writhing in agonies, which drove the blood through His pores, that it stood like sweat on His brow; and falling prostrate before His Heavenly Father, whose will He was ever so ready to do; praying, praying amidst the temptation of despair, and yet so humbly and meekly; praying in strains, whose every tone must have rent, in sympathy, each bosom in the hosts of Heaven: "O my Father, if it be possible, let this cup pass from me," and still willing to drink it, and drain it to the dregs: and all for *you*, for you and me, to benefit *us* and pay the penalty for *our* sins!—and shall we let Him die in vain?

The Son of God, stretched out upon the cross,

and raised between heaven and earth, between two thieves, the substitute of a murderer; a crown of thorns, which cruel mockery had wound upon His head, so deeply bowed under that curse from which He died to free the world; scorned and railed at by that people which had been the witnesses of His power and His doctrine, and sacrificed to their fury; His blood flowing drop by drop and staining the tree, His body and the ground; His life ebbing lower and lower, and the sins laid upon Him, pressing more and more upon His heart, until it broke, and forced from His dying lips the cry: "My God, my God, why hast thou forsaken me?" Yet never ceasing to love that world for whose sake He suffered; never ceasing to comfort mourning sinners; and though He could not move His nailed hands towards those He wished to bless, nor fold them in His prayer; still breathing His pardon over a rebellious world, and praying for His murderers: "Father, forgive them;" *till it was finished*, and all creation shuddered at the scene; the sun hid himself, the heavens clothed themselves with blackness, the earth did quake and the rocks rent, the graves were opened and the dead started from their sleep, as if the last day had come; till all was finished, and He bowed down His head and gave up the Ghost; till all Scripture was fulfilled, and the work of atonement for the sins of the world, for *your* sins, completed!

Man of the impenitent heart, behold your crucified Redeemer! Why His lingering death? Why His sufferings? Why did not nature rise up, and the elements engage in war with man to stay the unnatural deed? why did not legions of angels take their Master from the tree and pass through the ranks of His persecutors and execute vengeance upon them? why did not the Father interpose and remove that cloud of wrath above the cross and take Him up unto Himself in Heaven? *He died for you,* that *you* might live! And with this love that made Him bear and suffer unto death, He comes to move your heart of stone. That agonized cry from the cross is for your sins; that imploring look, so full of love and pity is on you, is for your heart, to soften it and break it in repentance, and call it back to Holiness and God and Heaven—

And will you let Him cry and will you let Him die in vain?

The fool hath said in his heart, there is no God.

PSALMS xiv. 1.

But why select such a text? Who cares what a fool saith? True! But, brethren, there are a great many fools in this world, and if all their voices be silenced man's conversation will be very limited. In one sense, the sense of the word to which I shall revert after awhile, all men belong to that class, for all are sinners. But beyond this, as the words of the wise are a guide into truth and holiness and righteousness, so the words of the fool may be a marsh-light that leads its followers astray, or a beacon-light to warn us off from sin and error. And in this way the words of the fool, quoted in the text, receive a weight of importance, a depth of meaning, a breadth of bearing, and become a source of results which go beyond all else.

I. *There is no God!* It is the secret of the fall, the fundamental fact from which is begotten the sinful life of man; if I might use a modern term, the "protoplasm" of all sin. This is God's own teaching of this Psalm, and underlying all the teaching of His word. The context makes this perfectly plain: "The fool hath said in his heart, there is no

God! They are corrupt, they have done abominable works, there is none that doeth good, they are all gone aside, they are altogether become filthy, there is none that doeth good; no, not one!" All, my brethren—the effects of that disbelief, which is embodied in the fool's declamation, "there is no God!" "They call not upon the Lord," is the closing description, the clinching fact with which the sin of man is driven back into its first cause—apostasy from God. I have often thought that all treatises on morals should be written from this point of view. Not infidelity as one of our sins, not as the effect of a sinful life, (though that strengthens and upholds the unbelief of man and develops it in its multiform manifestations,) but reasoning from the cause to its effects, starting with unbelief, with the apostasy from God, with the hopeless " without God," as our creed. A true system of moral philosophy would trace all the sins and errors of this fallen world, all the wickedness and wretchedness, the fear and doom of individual man, to this Scripture-truth, *unbelief*, the root of all sin. Just as before and with and after all physical phenomena stands the Creator, who called them into existence and guides them with His almighty hand; so before and with and after all moral and spiritual life, lies that one truth, the existence and the living presence of the personal God, who, at sundry times and in diverse manners, has revealed Himself to His rational and accountable creatures. Unbelief, the root of sin, the germ, the bud that contains the fruit of sin, *of all sin*, with all its innate penalty of corruption, suffering, wretchedness, and death of hope! It is not the secret of the introduction of sin, for unbelief is of the essence of sin, and the possibility of that sin is given in the free agency of man; but it lays open the secret of man's subsequent corruption and growing depravity. As that light, which, at the fiat of God, first electrified the chaotic masses of matter and began that course of arrangement, combination, collection, and co-ordination, of evolution if you choose, which ripened into the order and beauty of the heavens and the earth, which proclaim God's glory: so the light of truth, flowing from the same God, became the life and guide of the immortal soul. Blot out the light of these heavens and a darkened, freezing world ceases to exist. Turn from that light of God's truth—and darkness, corruption, moral and spiritual death must follow.

It is the grandest truth revealed and the key to the soul's history in life. "Without God—" no guide, no dependence, no higher feelings and aspirations, to hold up the image of God. "Without God,"—

all ultimate responsibility abolished. Can you do away with that? Without His revealed will, the basis of all morality taken away (for God's will is the only absolute arbiter of right and wrong); every sin is a sin against God, and hence its heinousness and fatal power.

Man's history begins with it. The first act of sin *followed* disbelief in God and His word. "Yea, hath God said, ye shall not eat of it, neither shall ye touch it, lest ye die?" and man believed the devil more than God, and plucked the forbidden fruit. Once remove that belief, and with it that responsibility, and man's will becomes the law and the creature his own God! Follow the outline of the history of the race. After having broken with God it was easy to break with man; and the first child born into this world dipped his hands in his brother's blood. All that remained was for man to break with himself and defile his own soul and body, his mind and conscience, in serving his own lusts. The wave of corruption flowed over the earth, and ever since has carried on its tide its guilty souls to ruin—" without God!" the curse of that life!

As we descend in the course of centuries and study the different epochs which mark the great outlines of nations: always, everywhere *materialism*, the development of this apostasy, the denial, not only of God, but of our own higher, God-like nature—has carried in its train, even amidst the splendours of an Augustan era, in whatever country or age it be found, socially or scientifically, the deeper fall of the race from its high and glorious destiny, unhumanized life, and left in lieu of the true man, to quote Augustin, "a splendid animal," and worse than a fallen angel. The failure of the old faith in any country, at any time, whatever God it was that was revealed in that old faith, in the East, in Greece, in Rome, in the Church of Christ Himself, was the downfall of the people, the failure of its calling. Of course, "without God," and no restraint upon the passions of the runaway soul; that, to sustain itself had to make the most of this life and sacrifice to it every higher hope and aim: "*seek ye first and only the things of this life*," (for there is nothing after,) is the necessary creed when the belief in God has failed. How fearful to trace this out in the life of the individual! Perhaps first a mere decline, till the soul gets used to it—lukewarmness, carelessness, worldliness, the thought of God inconvenient, troubling the stupor or frenzy which had seized it—until *habitual ungodliness* binds the soul to the ministry of a life of labor and sorrow for its three-score years and ten and no hope beyond, to the ministry of evil and the bondage of sin and fear and death. For boast as you may of that intellectual height which writes "no God" upon His handiwork, you cannot blot out that God; He is there, and the infidel and sinner know it. "Thou God seest me," is the confession wrung from convictions that lie deeper than the fictions and pretensions of the Godless soul, the handwriting on the wall which fills that soul with fear and torment.

Oh, brethren, away, from God!—it is the fall of the soul into sin. And thus falling away farther, ever farther away from God; lower, ever lower down into hopeless, determined infidelity, and deeper, ever deeper, into sin—what must be the end?

II. The fool hath said in his heart "there is no God!" — With the heavens above and its glories shining on us; with the earth around us and its marvels of beauty and blessings; with the revelations of power, wisdom, benevolence in our own complicated existence, and the demands of the mind and the cravings of the soul: *what an unnatural effort does it require*, what a pre-determined, conscious, studied and *defiant resolution*, not to see, not to hear, not to feel! to blind the understanding and stifle conviction and silence the voice of the heart; to blot out from all the name of God, and stultify man's reason by denying the cause of these effects!

Ordinary, common-sense and unsophisticated men never do so. It requires an effort for which we vainly seek an adequate cause, except in the determination to get rid of God and our responsibility to Him. I cannot put it in smoother words. What studies, what round-about ways, what fanciful premises, what life-long sophistries—at last to induce the mind even to listen to such philosophy! The greatest students of God's world, those who have created modern science, all found in the wonders of the eye and the ear, in the revelations of either the telescope or the microscope, *vestiges of the great Creator*. It requires an effort to deny them their witness to the existence, power, wisdom, living presence of God. The sphere of the mind must be lowered, conscience and consciousness must be put in a new and false training, before the result can be reached. — This is not the place nor am I the man to treat the question scientifically or philosophically, or whatever it may require to meet such tremendous efforts against nature and nature's convictions and nature's catechism. I appeal only to common sense and the convictions of every man's mind and the craving of every man's heart. "Out of nothing nothing can be made. Just as sure as anything *is*, *something has always been its cause, and that something is God.* If at any time in the flow of eternal ages, there was nothing, there would be nothing still."

The supposition of matter to be eternal is impossible; if there ever was a time when all was chaos, all would be chaos still. The first attribute of matter is *inertness*. There must be first a *moving cause*. The collocations and co-ordinations in matter deal the death-blow to all such atheism; and time enough, however brief, has passed to prove this to many of those who first started with these impossibilities. To deny the reasoning from effects to causes is useless. We are born to it, and from one fact to another the mind travels and finds causes for effects, the causes themselves becoming effects; on, on, the series grows, till the mind wearies, becomes bewildered, dizzy; and there is no rest till the basis of all is found in a great—*the great first cause*—GOD! There is no rest for the mind without this. We can believe in a self-existent God, (and all the world does believe and has believed in Him), but the interminable series of effects and causes, reaching back to *no end*—it is that materialism which, of all attempts of the metaphysical mind, has been and ever will be, the most unsatisfactory and the most degrading.

We must rest in the final cause—God. Call it unphilosophical as much as you please. No array of learned phraseology will ever change this postulate of the reasoning mind. It is the universal axiom.

That poet who has had the deepest insight into human nature and the aspirations of its lofty intellect, vainly introduces his hero studying the 1st chapter of St. John's Gospel (and, of course, misreading it) to solve the question: In the beginning was the 'Word'—no, no! the Word could not have such power. *The mind, the thought?* but that is not enough—it is the *force, the power!* more than one hundred years ago anticipating the shiboleth of the present day. But it gave his active mind no rest—no! it must be "in the beginning was the *deed*, the *act.*" And there he rested. Certainly. But back of that deed must stand the *doer*, and back of that act the *actor* or *agent;* and back of this creation he investigates, the *Creator!* I challenge any one to find a flaw in this common-sense argument. — And *what* a Creator!

Can you look upon the phenomena of this world and see how they all are suited and matched to each other, and supply each other's wants, and tally with the capacities contained in each? Can you pass on from world to world and see the reign of law and the perfect order, and symmetry with which all are moving, and the harmony from one end of creation to the other—such as made the poetic minds of all ages speak of "the harmony of the spheres"—and listen to the silent anthem which rises from all these countless creatures of Almighty power, and not bow in reverence; and behold design, intelligence, purpose in all? No architect, no worker, no God! I think the folly of infidelity reaches its acme, when it sneers superciliously at this argument from "design" as unphilosophical, unscientific.

Pass on, and take the higher manifestations of *inner life*, as much subjects of our cognizance and investigation as the physical phenomena of the world—*the cravings of the soul*, the demands, the necessities *of the heart—and will you give it a world without a God?*

All this glory, all this beauty, all these countless coincidences and mutual complements, this universal co-operation and harmony which thrill the human heart, and which human intellect copies and follows in the constructions of its own intelligent nature; that mind, that soul longing to rise to the Great Maker and sustainer of all, and seeking the face and heart that throb through the universe, as approachable and responsive (or it finds no peace and satisfaction,) and as the result: *a dead machine*, a "*perpetuum mobile*," without the motive act, without the guiding mind and without the sustaining power and life; all mere matter, mere matter, because we are determined to have nothing else; nothing beyond and above; though we must *unmaterialize matter* to explain its phenomena, suspend its inertness, ascribe to it attributes which do not belong to matter, and thus admit impossibility.

Ah, we must go beyond all this; and let us be forced—let the strictest advocates of mere materialism be forced at last to admit *a God*, a force, a thought behind it all; *is that the goal the soul of man seeks—must seek?* or there is no hope, no strength and relief and comfort; no future to speak of immortality, no love to meet the love that springs up in the heart as its most blessed possession, roaming through a universe of worlds and seeing nothing but matter, matter—spiritual death, death—no soul! no God to love us, no Christ to save us!

Oh, in the soul's life, what wants, what cravings! And where every atom finds its mate, and every tendency its help, no response to that undying cry of the soul? In joy no sympathy; in sorrow no consolation; in fear no relief; in hope no certainty; in sin no redemption; in death no eternal home! Going through all the wonders of flesh and blood—(for such they are without a soul,) and no Christ! Tell me not of your wisdom and philosophy; what can you give for the life, the hopes, the certainties of this living God and living Christ, that speaks to me from the Bible, and whispers its truths and consolations in my heart! That is not wisdom to bless a world to say, "There is no God!"

To feel life within, and vainly seek it without; to struggle against self and sin, and ask for help in vain; to suffer and pine, and no appeal for comfort. To sit day by day, and night by night, near the dying couch of my child, and find no response to my prayers from above; to wander in sin and seek to return, and no Father to welcome the returning prodigal; to be dying of life, the life of the soul, and no Redeemer, nothing to go to but a dead world! No God! no Christ!

Oh! let the wise of the earth keep their vaunted wisdom, which gives me a stone for bread, a blank for the promise of hope lying deep in my heart! *Give me* the foolishness of the child's faith, that knows and feels and says, *there is a God, there is a Christ!*

III. "*The fool hath said in his heart there is no God!*"

I come to my last point. Thus far I have, in the main, been giving you and arguing before you the common interpretation of this verse and its context in the Psalm. All is true, but I am sure *the special meaning of the text* goes far beyond it. We have not yet gotten at the pith and marrow of that word, not yet touched the nerve of it:

"The fool hath said in his heart, there is no God."

To me it is a proposition self-evident that the man who denies the existence of God, and with it all that flows from it, is a fool. Atheism is the most glaring, monstrous folly to the soul, that cannot deny its immortality, and has no data to deny its Maker and Redeemer. We do not want revelation, do not want the Bible, (that never wastes time in self-evident truths,) to tell us *that*, and tell it so solemnly. It is all involved in it, and there will be times when this aspect of the question is presented. But far above soars the real teaching of the text; far above, because much more intimately connected with the inner life of man and the necessary processes of his accountable existence. Far, deep into the soul, the heart of hearts, goes the teaching of my text.

Revelation is not necessary to prove the existence of God; but its great purpose is not only to teach us what sin is and its heinousness, but also that *sin is incompatible with belief in God;* for every sin is the result of unbelief, the denial, the rejection, the defiance of the living God!—

We are misled by the translation of our Bible; the terms "fool," "foolishness," "folly," have, in the Old Testament, *a moral* rather than intellectual meaning. They are equivalent to "sinner," "sinfulness," "sin." And here is the true teaching of the text: *The sinner* hath said in his heart there is no God! I have not time to stop to prove the correctness of this interpretation Go to your Bible, and from the book of Genesis on to the last book of the Old Testament, you will find that "folly" and "sin" are terms synonymous. "She has wrought folly in Israel," is said of the woman that sinned. "Do not thou this folly," is the vain appeal of the victim to her strong and overpowering foe. "My wounds stink and are corrupt, because of my foolishness." "Oh, God! Thou knowest my foolishness, and my sins are not hid from Thee." Such texts are scattered all over God's word.

The truest meaning of the text is, *the sinner* hath said in his heart there is no God! *The sinner; every sinner!* A man may hold many errors and wrong views, and suffer from his mistakes; but *sin* alone separates from God, for it dethrones Him, and denies His being and His reign. *Every sinner*, and *whenever a man sins*, even a Christian, when surprised into sin, is guilty of *saying in his heart*, "there is no God!" This shows how unbelief begets sin, how every sin cuts us loose from our relation to God Himself, and is in rebellion against Him.

And mind, he need not acknowledge it in words, need not proclaim it from the house-top, may keep very quiet about it and preserve the decorum of an outward creed and even profession; but *he hath said in his heart*, to himself, to quiet his fears, "Tush! shall God see?"—to stifle his conscience, to fight down his better Self, to sweep away his religious scruples. Determined to do wrong, to violate God's law, he persuades himself that God *is not*, certainly not present then, not there to take notice of it. He forgets Him when temptation surprises him. He lives in sin because he realizes not and tries *not to believe* in the omnipresence of a living sin-avenging God; yet who, upon repentance and resistance to sin, is the sin-forgiving Saviour.

Here it is, and the plain teaching of this text: Committing sin, living in sin—incompatible with the belief in God! Every sinner practically an atheist, every sin the denial of our God!

Just think a moment. There is your knowledge of right and wrong; then comes the temptation! Could you yield to it if *you saw God* standing by you, and your Saviour's wounds bleeding again, being crucified afresh by you? Could you sin, would you have the moral or the physical force or courage, if you *saw* God? If you had the faith which sees Him, sees Him in His purity and holiness, the tables of the eternal law of righteousness in His hands, and calling to you and claiming you as His? With the threat of His vengeance upon the sinner, hell yawning upon him with its untold terrors? With the promise of all-sufficient grace to the penitent who resists and has "respect to God," heaven open for every one that believes! Is it possible to sin with such a belief? No, we sin because, as we flee away from God, hide ourselves from Him like Adam, forget Him: we think that puts Him off from us, and He will not see us and take account of us. Every sin is a denial of God's presence and holiness.

Here is the true gauge:

Does the drunkard proclaim his faith in God while he quaffs the fatal poison? Ah! I have known him in his frenzy to say he would take it if a gun were pointed at him; but it was all a lie! A false boast! Why, I have known him to stop when *I* came in the room. Like every sinner he can stop, whenever he has dread of others, sufficient faith in the obstacle to his sin. He indulges it when no one sees him but his boon companions in the same sin with him; he shuns the public eye, and all are heeded but God, because he fools himself with the falsehood, "there is no God!"

Will the adulterer indulge his vile practice when

the eye of a witness is upon him? does he not seek the darkness and secrecy of the night, and exclude all that could possibly reveal his sin—"wipe his mouth" and boldly step before the world that has not watched him and say: "I have done no wickedness!" But unblushingly he sins in the sight of the all-seeing God, because he does not see Him present, does not believe that sin is recorded by Him, does not fear Him, whom he does not believe. "*Je me damne mais je ne peux faire autrement,*" said the lascivious monk. It was a lie; he could, he can stop, stop for every interruption; and would stop for damnation if it really broke upon him in fact, as it should have been present to his faith.

Or the murderer, the thief—why he looks around to see if no one is near, seeks the cover of darkness or the lonely hour, fears everybody but God; does he believe in that righteous God then?

The covetous—ah! I know of no one who so diligently tries to escape the public eye, who tries so eagerly to appear the very opposite of what he is; because he fears the most scornful contempt of his fellow-creatures, should they see him grinding as a slave at Mammon's wheel. God sees him; sees all; but the love of gold has blinded the miser that he cannot see, cannot love, cannot believe in God.

My brethren, *could they commit, could any commit*

the act of sin, if they believed in Him? If by that faith which is the evidence of things not seen, the substance of things *hoped for* or *feared, if by such faith they saw Him?*

No; impossible! Sin blots out God from our presence and consciousness, and nothing saves from the power of sin but faith; faith that alone has power to make God present to us, real, felt in the soul, to bless or to curse. —

And thus we come back to the point from which we started—disbelief, unbelief, forgetfulness of God, " without God in the world,"—the root of sin.

All sin: Godlessness—without God; ungodliness—not conformed to His image; unbelief—in its manifestations of profaneness and irreligion; denial—of His claims and authority; rebellion—against His laws; ingratitude—for His blessings; abuse—of His mercies; abuse of our highest power as free agents—even to serve God, the sons of God!

All involved in the sin of unbelief. It is this which makes it sin and makes it so exceedingly sinful. Oh! my brethren, is it not true that such is the life, the course, the reasoning of all who are not Christians, not believing in God the Father, and Jesus Christ, whom He has sent? *and is it not foolishness?*

You may believe you are sinning in secret, and

your sin shall not find you out. *Stop! Here is God*, who seeth in secret, sees you now and here, sees your heart and what is in it! — You may wear the cloak of fairness and decency, and try to make amends by charities and good actions which cost you nothing, not the darling sin of your heart. *Stop! Here is God*, and His judgment is with Him upon every soul of man that maketh a lie, and sins in defiance of His law.

Will you rush into hell-fire that is before you, rather than cut off the right hand and pluck out the right eye that offends? because you do not see it and fool yourself into the denial of all retribution?

But brethren, *here is Christ;* He speaks in this very psalm, and speaks of His salvation which comes out of Zion.

Here is Christ to call you, save you, love you, to redeem you from the power of sin, to help you to come off conqueror and more than conqueror. He shed His blood to cancel your guilt. He gave Himself to win your heart.

To Him take the heart of unbelief, and as you see Him dying for you on the cross and praying for your poor soul "Father forgive them," and opening Heaven for the returning prodigal, for all that believe: *arise and live!* The darkness is passed, light is sprung up! Arise and live in that light, a ransomed sinner by faith in Jesus Christ; *there is no cure of sin but that—*

"*Thou God seest me*"—the beacon!

"*Lord save or I perish*"—the escape!

"*I can do all things through Christ that strengthens me*"—the triumph!

What fruit had ye then in those things, whereof ye are now ashamed? for the end of those things is death.

ROM. vi. 21.

Few doctrines have been so much abused as the great and precious doctrine of justification by faith. The Apostle had seen it himself in several of his churches, and his prophet-eye discerned how, throughout the ages of the Church, the adversary would take his stand here and ruin souls by disconnecting faith and works, justification and sanctification; and on the specious plea that all is of grace, and pardon the gift of God, irrespective of works: delude people into the belief that it was perfectly immaterial how they lived, that it was useless to strive for holiness, inasmuch as grace alone would do the work. Yea, that the glory of the Gospel and the triumph of Christ would be all the greater, the greater the amount and depth of our sinfulness; for the Apostle himself had said, "Where sin abounded grace did much more abound."

Few, indeed, will be found who would commit themselves boldly to such views, which conscience tells us are profane and presumptuous, and disgraceful even in the sight of man. But I know also, that few are entirely free from a leaning towards such views, that too many are ready to neglect their own part in the work and cease striving, in the hope that under the Gospel dispensation things will not be taken so strictly, and that the grace of Christ will make up for our deficiencies. Ah! how many, brethren, whose conscience smites them for their inconsistencies and backslidings, for their lukewarmness and coldness in Christ's service; or at least whose conscience would smite them but for their self-absolution just on that ground? who allow their interest in religion to take a subordinate place, are satisfied with merely hanging on, whilst they rush with eager relish into the various occupations and dissipations of the world!—and yet who think they are Christians and are perfectly safe, and trust to the grace of Christ and God's mercy in Him! Is it not clear that they not only put asunder what God has joined together; *i. e.*, separate justification and sanctification, but join together what God has put asunder—faith in Christ with love of the world and the service of sin.

But to come to the argument of the Apostle. The great epistle to the Romans is his unanswerable declaration of the Christian doctrine of justification by faith, and yet his protest against all unrighteousness of life. In his first five chapters he speaks only of justification, and clearly proves that this is not by the deeds of the law, that it must be of grace through faith. He now brings up the question himself, which secretly rises as a hope in the carnal mind, "We are saved without works, without the law—why be so anxious about sin?" The Apostle knew that this train of thought would rise secretly in the carnal mind, and he meets it himself. What shall we say then? "Shall we continue in sin, that grace may abound?" God forbid! he cries in answer. "How shall we that are dead unto sin live any longer therein?" Here is his first argument: "We that are dead to sin!" This cannot mean dead to the power, the temptation, the baneful influence of sin upon his heart and life; for if this was the condition of the Christian neither you nor I could indulge the hope of being Christians. The Apostle himself, in the next chapter, confesses this power and influence of sin, sin dwelling in him—"when I would do good evil is present with me; the good I would that I do not, but the evil that I would not that I do." No; according to the connexion of the whole argument of the Apostle and the true condition of the Christian, it means death to the condemning, death-bringing power of sin! From this the Christian is freed, his guilt is pardoned; all that are baptised in Christ are baptized into His death; *i. e.*, are declared partakers of

His death. We, by faith, acknowledge it as our death; we accept it, take it as the expiation of our guilt; we are baptised into His death, so that henceforth our sins being atoned for, we go free—in other words, we believe in Christ for justification on the strength of that death He suffered for us, and the benefits of which we take to ourselves, and have sealed to our souls as God's promise, in the sacrament. But shall we, thus freed, continue in sin? Do we think God gave His son to save those who remain impenitent? To bring us pardon without making us better? To abolish the guilt of those who are perishing in the worse plague of sin? for guilt is only imputation, but sin is the reality. Why the whole would be of no use or purpose, were it not that those who thus are freed from the curse of guilt should rise in newness of life, should not henceforth serve sin but live unto God, be changed from sinners to saints. This is the very object of the Gospel, the leading thought in Christ's death. " He gave Himself for us;" *i. e.*, freed us from the death-sentence of the law for our sin and guilt by His atonement: *not* that we should remain sinners, but "to redeem us from all iniquity," the power and habit of sin, and "purify unto Himself a peculiar people, zealous of good works."

Here then we see the connection between justification and sanctification; and how *the first is given to us for the sake of the other.* The very object of His atonement is, that the soul thus redeemed from the death-doom of sin should rise towards God in a new life of holiness and love. The benefits of the Gospel are not limited to the removal of this sentence, this striking off the fetters of the prisoner and bringing him the deed of release; its benefits go with him through life, and become grace to him by which he learns to live unto God and become meet for his heavenly home.

And can the sinner continue to cavil and say "grace," "under grace?" Why worry about the law and its demands if we are under grace? Such a view involves a contradiction in terms. What is the reign of grace which Christ has established? Is it a dispensation which spares sin or which spares the sinner? Brethren, the sinner cannot be spared, while sin is spared, for death is the wages of sin, and even the mercy of God cannot undo this law. If the sinner is to be spared, there must not only be a just and sufficient satisfaction, such as is offered in the atonement and is ours, if by faith we are buried with Christ; but his sin must be done away with, it can no longer be spared, it must be crucified as Christ Himself, the sin-bearer, was crucified for us; it must be eradicated. And this is the true grace of God, that the sinner, who through faith in Christ has died with Him to *the doom of guilt*, now in the new life to which he is raised, learns to renounce, subdue, mortify, overcome *sin*, that it should no longer reign over him; that in the Gospel of Christ motives and strength and means are given us to maintain the upper-hand against sin; and though sometimes, perhaps often, beaten down and never perfect, yet under the dispensation of His grace, to hold on to the truth, and run our course for heaven and heavenly-mindedness in that liberty with which Christ has made us free, till we have gained the victory, *the victory of grace.*

This grace cannot co-exist with wilful indulgence in sin, or even the careless service of sin. Where the one reigns the other must be cast out. When one triumphs, the other must yield. *And thus we can know where we stand.*

This is the second argument of the Apostle:— " Know ye not that to whom ye yield yourselves servants to obey his servants ye are to whom ye obey, whether of sin unto death or of obedience unto righteousness." " By their fruits ye shall know them," saith the Saviour.

And now, after this course of reasoning, the

Apostle in conclusion adds his last argument in the form of an appeal to the consciousness and experience of the individual Christian. "What fruit had ye in those things whereof ye are now ashamed?" The Apostle merely asks the question, feeling sure the verdict could be nothing but unprofitableness, shame, death;—a crushing argument, and he does not wait for an answer; he only adds, "*and their end is death.*" But may not we press home this truth? This is just what His ministers have to do; we take the suggestions of the inspired writers and apply them to the various, but real and individual cases before us.

What fruit had ye then? This question is addressed, in the first place and emphatically to Christians who have been made to feel their sin, and seek something better; who have some experience in both paths, the path of the impenitent and the path of the believer. Only those who can compare the two states, their relative joys and sorrows, and their respective fruits, are enabled to give a full answer. Yet I doubt if there are any who are entirely devoid of such knowledge. All know enough of the truth, all have cherished better desires, not to feel the curse that is in this life of sin. Believe me, nothing is more certain than this: as godliness has two promises, the promise of the life that now is and that which is to come, so sin has its threatening not only for eternity, but also here. It is not only that *its end is death, in life itself* it has its curse, and its fruits even here are Sodom-apples, fair in their deceitful outside but rottenness within. Sin itself is the worst curse under which man can lie. St. Paul calls it the sting of death; ah, and it is no less "the sting of life."

We can appeal to the impenitent, the unbelieving, the man who openly or secretly serves sin. Are you willing to tell us your experience and point out the fruit of your lives? Have they rewarded you for the price you paid for them? Did you get, I will not say, the worth of your souls, but the worth of your labour? Are you satisfied with the devil's wages?

Suppose we bring it home by some leading illustrations. Take the victims of sensual indulgence. I mean in the largest sense—self-indulgence, excess, intemperance, living in pleasure, living for the pleasures and gratifications of earth and the carnal mind. Has there been no alloy in their gratification, no wretchedness of self-condemnation, no shunning the public eye and hiding from the scrutiny of the world? no loathing of their very pastimes, for which they felt they were bartering their better portion? Ah! you have spent your strength for the gratification of *the animal* in you, and that lower animal nature may have reaped its fruit! But is it the fruit which can rejoice and satisfy the *rational, immortal creature?* You have had your reward, but it was not what you bargained for—your wretched reward of sin here in this fleeting world: surfeit, remorse, dissatisfaction; a painful, desolate void; the craving, the irresistible cravings of your better nature starved, unsatisfied, degraded—with a Tantalus-thirst for blessings that you have trampled under foot, and can never, never have as you are. They followed you through all the changing scenes of your ever-more-failing life, and brought shame upon you as the fruit of your sin *here*, and "*the end eternal death.*"

Or, take the covetous—mind you, I speak not of the man to whom God has given wealth, or who reaps the legitimate fruits of proper and over painstaking industry—I speak of the covetous—all understand the difference. It is not money which the Apostle declares to be the root of all evil, but "the love of money," the all-absorbing love, the supreme and reckless pursuit of it. The covetous—oh, God! for the poor earnings of a few years, to stifle every generous feeling, to narrow the heart, to live in slavery to the passing, deceitful gains, so that it is not they that are yours, but *you are theirs;* and to degrade man, made in the image of God, into the timid, hungry, selfish idolater of wealth? What is your fruit? Let the wrinkles on your brow answer, let your cares and anxieties witness for you; your fears, your dependence on those things which perish in the using! your love for nothing but what you must give up—certainly when you die. Ah! the man that lives only to get rich—years pass upon years, cares multiply, tender and generous feelings are crushed, the world despises them, the poor curse them, laughing heirs are waiting for their death. dissipated sons go to ruin in hope of their coming fortune—*and your fruit?* After twenty, thirty, fifty years of labour and care and actual slavery to the most deceitful, cruel master—perhaps you get wealth, (and yet how few get it!) to build you a fine house and live in great style and shine in society—*how long?* Do you not know how one sudden crash may prostrate all your earthly prosperity, and give wings to your riches to fly away and leave you poor—leave you nothing but your unquenched thirst for what you have lost? Or, keep your stores, and save them from the general wreck, let them remain to you a few years *and you are gone!* you *must leave them.* "We brought nothing into this world and we can carry nothing out." Is this success? the success of a life of labour and toil? Even society, poor and unchristian as it is in many respects, despises the man that claims the esteem of his fellows merely because he was smart and clever, perhaps mean and hard-hearted enough to coin money or try to do so! And at what price? Every noble feeling stifled, every hope of better things vanished; and all the time *God sees thee*, and the hour is coming when he shall say "give an account of thy stewardship"—and any moment His voice may go forth—"thou fool, this night thy soul shall be required of thee."

And I might speak of the uncharitable and of the revengeful, of the victims of temper, envy. Unloved, unblessed, with a Mordicai at the gate to embitter their every possession, with no friend to sympathize, no hand to clasp, they pass through life. Is that the fruit ye laboured for?

I speak of any and all who do not set God before their eyes, but live unto themselves and their idols, the lust of the eye and the lust of the flesh, and the pride of life. Brethren, we can get none of them to tell us the fruit of their labours; aye, not one of them would confess to his idols. They are too much ashamed of them, and yet they live on and ripen for that final death, which is but the last fruit their sowing to sin brings forth.

Ah! and even if the sinner should never realize the curse that is on him here, can he boast of the joys which are the privilege and the holy aspiration of the Christian? the peace of heart, the knowledge of God's love, the communion with Christ, the certainty of help in every hour of need, the assurance that all things shall work together for his good? Can he boast of that high and holy calling which is laid upon the Christian and which grace enables him to follow after, to glorify God, to serve Him here on earth, to set forth the beauty of holiness, to become to others an angel of mercy by leading them to the Saviour and doing them good? I say, *if a man's life does not bring forth these fruits it is a failure*, not worth living for; toiling, toiling from morning till night, day after day, for the perishing baubles of the world, for the fickle applause of others, for the gratification of only our lowest wants, our animal appetites and passions, indulgence in which but sinks us lower in the scale of rational beings. There is but one fruit that is blessed, "the fruit unto holiness and the end everlasting."

And beloved, that is not all. Yes, if conversion freed us from the fruits of sin? But no, "those things of which we are now ashamed" follow us into our Christian life; their remembrance often darkens the doors of free grace to our souls, falling again under fearful conviction; or, what is worse, they have given us *habits* which will spring up again in after life and become thorns and scourges in our side, and surround us with temptation and difficulties, and afford the adversary opportunities to assail us. Oh, God! if the secret life of Christians were known we would know something of this, something of the struggles caused by the former service of sin, of the former lust starting up, faintly at first, haunting us perhaps in dreams, introducing itself into our thoughts, filling the imagination till the soul is led on farther and farther—oh, where shall it end? "Of whatsoever a man is overcome, of the same is he brought into bondage." Is not this the reason of almost every backsliding? And what but the grace of God can free us from the bitter taste of such fruits of sin, "of which you are now ashamed?" Ah! ashamed? Would you have your fellow-Christian know your thoughts and your spiritual troubles? You are ashamed even to confess them to God, to yourselves often; yet the heart knoweth its own bitterness, and sometimes it must find vent for the pent-up feelings of sorrow and anguish, and the bitterest and most humbling and startling confessions are poured into the pastor's ears. God grant this self-knowledge may lead every one more and more to Christ and keep him humble and zealous, lest all his hopes should prove a delusion, for "the end of these things is death."

And is it not this after all, this hankering after the idols of the world, this exposure to our former lusts and their selfish aspirations which draws us away from the cross of Christ and the self-denying love the Christian life enjoins? is it not this which causes all the inconsistencies, all the faults of Christians? If a man is dead and cold and lukewarm, if he talks lightly of sin, if his thoughts and conversation give not witness of his nearness to Christ; why is this? but because he is reaping the fruit of corruption, the harvest of his own sowing to the flesh, his heart is turned back to the sins from which he was purged; he forgets that

> God from the curse has set us free,
> To make us pure within;
> Nor did He send His Son, to be
> The minister of sin.

What fruit have we then, as professing Christians, in those things of which we must feel ashamed in the sight of God, ashamed at the thought of Christ and all He did and suffered for us, ashamed in the estimation of others and before our own conscience, and ashamed in view of the last issue: Death and final retribution; eternal shame or eternal glory!

Ah! beloved, the two roads are before you with their termination of death or life; the road of sin and death, the road of liberty and life! Arise and wash away thy sin, for Christ has died to set us free from its condemnation, and Christ is alive to free us from its power. Follow on to make your calling and election sure; for without holiness no man shall see the Lord! Follow on, for ye are not under the law but under grace. God worketh in you to will and to do, therefore "work out your own salvation with fear and trembling."

Persevere and conquer, for eternity stands before you; and behold it is Christ that calls unto you from heaven, "Come unto me and be ye saved all the ends of the world!" Oh! may you hear and resolve now! *But remember the terms,* "Be thou faithful unto death, and I will give thee a crown of life."

> *I shall be satisfied when I awake with Thy likeness.*
>
> PSALMS xvii. 15.

"I shall be satisfied?" And is this the language of the Christian? Is not his a present satisfaction? A state of peace and joy in the Holy Ghost, of joy and peace in believing, even here on earth? How many sweet texts have we treasured in our hearts, how many sermons have been preached to us, how many books, perhaps, or tracts have we read which turned on this very point, and contrasted the unhappy, the changeful and unsatisfactory state of the worldling with that of the Christian—happy amidst all the trials and troubles of this life, enduring through all the changes and chances of our pilgrimage on earth, satisfying all his wants and meeting all the demands he can make on time or on eternity—as he knows and rejoices in the knowledge, that mercy has come to him, unchangeable like the love of God that makes all things his. "All things are yours," for above life and death and the world "God is yours;" not *shall* be, but *is* yours *now*, and "Christ is yours," your ever-present help, your ever-living Saviour.

And yet here is one of a truly Christian mind,

a man after God's own heart, the inspired Psalmist, who still feels a want, still gives witness to his longing for more by consoling his aspiring soul with the hope, "I shall be satisfied when I awake with Thy likeness."

Let us understand this.

There is a satisfaction which belongs to the Christian here on earth, which is perfect and complete; the satisfaction which flows from the gift of pardon and adoption into God's family in Christ. I know Christians may not have this actual sense of pardon alike, nor any realize it at all times. But I do say that it is the right and privilege, aye more, the duty of all. The moment we believe in Christ that moment we are justified, *pardon now is ours, God is reconciled.* We are His children by adoption and grace, and we have no right to doubt the faithfulness of His promises. If you have really trusted your soul to Christ, if you really cling to Him as your only help and Saviour, rely upon His merits and love and grace, then know that pardon is yours, *is yours now;* that you are a member of Christ, *are so now;* not that you may become one hereafter; know that you have already entered the kingdom of heaven and eternal life. "He that hath the Son hath life;" not shall have it hereafter. "There is now no more condemnation for them that are in

Christ Jesus." You are the members of a household, against which the gates of hell shall not prevail. You are God's and He is yours, who will never leave you nor forsake you, under whose gracious government you can be perfectly happy; yours " His grace all-sufficient," yours " His strength according to your days." And know that for you death has lost its sting and the grave been robbed of its victory. Your very tears and trials of earth are but the child's portion of discipline, testimonials of your heavenly Father's faithfulness and love for you; and "neither life nor death, nor angels nor principalities, nor powers, nor things present nor things to come, nor height, nor depth, nor any other creature shall be able to separate you from the love of God which is in Christ Jesus our Lord." These are exceedingly precious and important truths. They are the present blessings which God has bestowed upon you. They are deeded to you in His holy word, and you have no right to say that you believe in Christ and have no other hope but Him, but still doubt that He has pardoned you and that God has actually accepted you. The same faith by which you call upon Christ for salvation and give up all to Him, the same faith demands of you to assume these blessings for you on the strength of God's word. The grace of pardon and justification are ours, they cannot be made more perfect, not even in heaven; our guilt is washed away, God's justice is appeased, we are admitted into His presence—not yet while the veil of this earthly life hangs over us, face to face, but as really, as savingly, as presently, by faith! It is not with regard to these that we may say, "I shall be satisfied."

But pardon and justification are not the only graces which are bestowed on the believer in Christ. Besides guilt and condemnation we are bearing the load of corruption and our sinful nature, and to overcome this we need the grace of holiness and sanctification. We must stand not only in the righteousness of Christ, but also in His will. Without this there could be no heaven for us, we would not be meet for its blessed life, not in the condition to enjoy its glories. "Without holiness no man shall see the Lord!" — But here, too, the Gospel, and the Gospel only, gives us the required satisfaction; the victory over sin is just, the "victory of our faith."

The difference is this: our justification is complete the moment we give up contending with God in our own name, and approach Him as sinners, who trust themselves to Christ. But sanctification is of a gradual development, it is the growth of the Christian on earth. Freed from the guilt that drove us from the presence of God, we unlearn our former sinfulness and are in the school of Christ, to be made holy and meet for the kingdom of heaven. We have entered that kingdom actually by faith, but we enter it as those who are under the teaching of Christ, to be governed only by His law, to adopt His will as ours, surrender our will to Him, and strive to be like Christ. And fully satisfied can we only be, when we have learned this lesson, when we have reached this perfection of our regenerate nature.

And now we may understand how the Psalmist, whose life was emphatically one of faith and entire dependence on Christ; who, through faith, could rise (as we learn from his hymns) from all his sorrows and trials, and was enabled even to glory in tribulation and sing songs in the darkest night; how he who never doubted the pardoning and helping grace of his Saviour, who was perfectly satisfied when thinking of God's willingness to pardon and Christ's ability to save to the uttermost; who in his deepest distresses could look up to Him with confidence, and after his worst falls, cry "Lord, I am thine, save me!" how he—when struggling after the bright example of Christ's holiness, and feeling the fearful throes of the enemy in his own carnal nature, as arrayed against the desires and resolves and energies of his better self, which had been born in him of God—how he could feel how much he yet lacked to be complete in sanctification; and from a heart overflowing with love for the Saviour and hanging on Him as his all in all, would long for the time when self should be entirely conquered, sin overcome, the old Adam left behind, and Satan deprived of his prey; and his will, freed from all ungodly influences, be entirely identified with the will of Christ, his whole nature not only regenerated by faith, but perfected through holiness into the likeness of Christ.

Now we may understand, too, the blessedness even of the struggling and agonized believer, who is so often cast down in his heavenward course and suffers from his spiritual foes and the sin which so easily besets him, yet who even then believes, and by faith knows, that he shall get the victory and come off more than conqueror through Him that loved him, and that when awakening from the fitful and the sadly chequered dream of life he shall "awake in the likeness of his Master."

Oh! my brethren, we cannot think too seriously of this. We cannot put up too high the standard of purity and love and godliness which we must pursue. *It is nothing less than to be like Christ!* to reflect His image as He when He was on earth, clothed in the rags of humanity, reflected the image of God. Thank God, we are not saved for our righteousness, but for Christ's! In our helpless state of sin and condemnation we must flee to Him for help, lay hold of His gift of pardon for all our sins, trust in His blood which cleanseth from every sin. But then, out of this very love for Him, though approaching Him in deepest humility and with the prayer of the publican, yet like the Apostle, we must press on towards the mark, "the mark which is the full stature of the measure of Christ." He who does not seek for it, he who does not strive to be like Christ, has none of His spirit, is no true believer. Oh! the longings of the true Christian for more grace! Who that has looked back over his life has not cause to mourn that he has advanced so little, made so little progress, whilst heaven and earth appealed to him by all that is dear and sacred, and whilst his own heart was urging him on, to follow Christ and be like Him? Oh! the tenderness of the true and loving Christian, whose conscience smites him for every short-coming and every failure in thought, emotion, word, and deed! All these are sorrows of the true Christian, brethren, and accompany us through life as we gain a further knowledge of Christ; but they cannot, cannot cast us down from our hopes which are placed, not upon *our* righteousness and our attainments, but upon Christ, and Him alone. Oh! if we can go to Him, even after years of struggles and labours, with the humbling confession of our unprofitableness, go to Him with the prayer, " Lord, I believe; help Thou mine unbelief," He will not cast us out, He will strengthen our hopes that rest on Him; and after all our struggles and conflicts with an evil heart and a sinful world and a deadly foe, after all our failures and all our partial successes, still keep alive in us both the desire and the certain hope of final success, and enable us to take comfort in the thought, " I shall be satisfied when I awake with Thy likeness." —

But can *we*, dare *we* cherish this hope? Can we hope to awake in the likeness of Christ; that is, wholly sanctified, holy as He is holy? If there is a heaven for us, it can be only on this condition. — There is no presumption in this assertion. We go to our graves reconciled and pardoned in the blood of Christ. But we must be holy as Christ is holy; that is, our whole will must be His, and His only; our whole spiritual life identified with Him—or heaven cannot be for us! And now here we are so imperfect, and our thoughts and words and actions so unworthy of the complete Christian's name, and even our best works, if sifted either in the motive or their extent, tainted or insufficient. How can we hope to pass at once from this state of imperfection into one of glory; for to be with Christ and to be like Him is glory.

The solution is not difficult. Justice is appeased, that we can understand. Christ has borne our sins and intercedes availingly for His own, and no purgatorial fire is to cleanse the soul from guilt. — But how is it with holiness? Beloved, there is in this life a conflict going on in the Christian; the new man created in him by the spirit of God, is indeed created in righteousnes and after the image of God. This is its very essence. This new-born spirit is set upon Christ, and in its true nature living to Him and following after Him. But he is opposed by the old man, the carnal nature, with which here he is united and surrounded by the evil and tempting influences of sin and a sinful world. A strife, a deadly battle goes on between them, and at times the better spirit seems to fall before the powerful assailants. And as long as he thus divides the dominion of the soul with the carnal nature, and is exposed to all that abets this, he may often be forced to exclaim, "Oh! wretched man that I am!" Often he may complain that he suffers from the law of the flesh that is in him; yet he struggles on, and Christ enables him to stand in the evil day, and having done all, to stand.

I appeal to every Christian if in his heart of hearts, if in the deepest depths of his soul, there is not Christ set up as his Saviour and King—if the most earnest desire of his whole being is not turned to Him, and how he knows no greater glory than to live to Christ, and how he is determined, with every imperfection upon him, and every difficulty around him, rather to die than not be a Christian; rather to lose all than his hold on Christ and the hope of being like Him, and glorifying Him in life or death. I appeal to every Christian for the truth of this; for where this spirit is not found there is no Christian spirit. But where it is found, the struggle may indeed be hard, and the issue at times apparently doubtful; the battle is raging, the conflict may be fierce, and many a weak moment may surprise him and many a fault be committed; but the new heart is there, the new man, the Christ-born man is there, hampered and distressed by what is really foreign to him, but true to his Master in his bias, his resolves, his aspirations, his prayers, his aims, his hopes, his fears! *Then death steps in!* And that moment which buries the impenitent sinner with all the curses of guilt and corruption upon him, comes as a deliverer to the believer. — You all believe that with death our sorrows are ended, our cares finished, our tears wiped away; a great change, brethren, and a real one. But it is as true that the reign of imperfection then is over, the old man perishes with all his sins; the carnal nature drops off with the temptations and helps of a world, partially in the grasp of Satan; and freed from the body of death, the new man soars aloft and finds his true centre of gravitation unchangeably, and forever and ever, in the heart and holiness of Christ! All that the new man was on earth he is now. It is not a new life, but life, begun on earth, is continued in heaven; but what was begun in weakness and mixed with sin, now rises in strength, as an atmosphere encloses him which has not known sin; and what we might call the natural propensities and functions of the new man, born of the spirit, now develop in perfect harmony, as sin and temptation and imperfections are forever gone. The new man starts from the evil dream of life while in a world that lieth in evil, and is satisfied as he wakes in the likeness of Christ!

Ah! here is the great characteristic of the Christian! his true aspiration: Christ in him the hope of glory! the glory: *not* of being seated among thrones and dominions, of wearing a crown and receiving the honours of heaven—the glory of being like Christ, holy and pure, perfect as God is perfect!

Here is perhaps the highest test of the Christian! When will he be satisfied? What is his highest hope? *Not*, beloved, that he escapes hell and gets to heaven; *not* that he shall be rewarded there for his labours and self-denials here, that he shall be compensated for forgoing the pleasures of earth and time by the glory and bliss of eternity; *not* that angels welcome him with songs of rejoicing and the arches of heaven ring with triumphal shouts; that he shall see the glorious city of God, and the tree of life, and the sea of crystal, and the golden streets of the new Jerusalem.

No! all this was his already, while on earth—his by faith! all this and more than this! all these and greater things: even repentance and love and godly aspirations, the presence and communion with the Father and the Son, and the glory of purifying himself even as Christ is pure; the happiness of loving poor, sinful, fallen men for Christ's sake, and perhaps bringing to them, as Christ did, the truth and comfort of the Gospel, and relieving aching hearts and soothing wounded spirits and winning souls for heaven; all was his here below!

One thing he lacked, one thing only which made earth imperfect for the Christian and his happiness incomplete. For as long as it is God's will, he is content to walk by faith and not by sight; and apart from his indwelling sin, has no right to choose between serving God on earth, or serving Him in heaven. *One thing alone was missing; perfect holiness*—and oh! he lives on earth in the hope, and he descends into the grave with the assurance, and he rises to heaven with the shout:

"I shall be satisfied when I awake in Thy likeness!"

Brethren, I count not myself to have apprehended: but this one thing I do, forgetting those things which are behind, and reaching forth unto those things which are before, I press toward the mark for the prize of the high calling of God in Christ Jesus.

PHIL.. iii. 13, 14.

There are few texts, which to me as a struggling disciple after holiness, bring greater comfort and encouragement. It is a confession so thoroughly human, portraying my own humiliating experience, and yet pointing me to the highest exercise of human powers and every godly energy, that it seems to be written especially for me and such as me.

I confess that when I think of the many drawbacks to a spiritual course, the humiliating experiences which force us continually to cry for forgiveness of all our "sins, negligences and ignorances," I cannot but feel some consolation when I see how even the greatest saints are exposed to the same exercises and pass through the same trials; their very confessions of insufficiency and shortcomings bring encouragement to my soul, and teach me that I am but suffering what all must go through, who pass from the state of natural corruption to the life in

God. And when I see them rise superior to everything and advance, I feel encouraged as by witnesses to my own triumph; and I mark their course and the means of their success and weapons of their warfare, and "go and do likewise." It is thus that these words of the Apostle become so unspeakably dear and valuable to me; become the rule by which I determine my own course: "forgetting those things which are behind, and reaching forth to those things which are before, I press toward the mark for the prize of the high calling of God in Christ Jesus."

There *is* a negative part of our work as Christians; there is a past replete with guilt and sin, with corruption and error and wretchedness, a past of bondage and fear of death; and we must be delivered from that. At the different stages of our progress this may assume different forms. It is an unlearning, a striving against, a renouncing, a continued warfare.

But when we are most taught by the grace of God, and have best learned how in Him alone is our strength, then we will know that the most powerful weapon of defence against all the assaults and difficulties which have impeded our cause is, "forgetting the things which are behind"—committing them all trustingly into the hands of our Redeemer, and assuming that He has delivered us from them; and that as long as we look to Him, and follow Him, and press on after Him, we are really redeemed from their curse and power. Believe me, brethren, this most efficient mode of seeking deliverance from our spiritual bondage and condemnation is the true, the needful policy for all. Forgetting the difficulties and sins and hindrances of your natural life; assuming and trusting that Christ is able and willing to remove, and actually does remove them, and takes charge of them for you: cease making your whole Christian life a warfare against what has kept you from Christ, a resistance against the besetting sins of your life. Cast them aside, as the same Apostle says; cast them into the hands of the Saviour, and feel that you are free to enter upon the positive course of living to his praise and glory. Go not back into the dark caverns of the past; do not continually conjure up the spectres of your guilt, your sinfulness, weakness and insufficiency—but look ahead! look to Him! follow Him and concentrate all your efforts upon *the course before you*, the course of a Christian life and obedience as God's dear children. Herein you shall find the alone remedy for all your failings; hereby you shall learn how we come off more than conquerors through Him that loved us.

This, our fleeing from the mere conflict against sin, our escaping from the low grounds of a miserable defensive warfare into the upper regions of aggressive, growing holiness, into the steady obedience of what Christ would have us do now and forever—this I conceive to be the true secret of the Christian life and Christian success.

What, then, have we to forget, brethren?

1. *Our guilt!* and this I hold to be the lowest lesson learned. The reluctance of going to Christ and taking His promises and invitation to ourselves because of the consciousness of our guilt is the first thing to be overcome and forgotten! We cannot be Christians without it! "Oh, I am such a sinner; I dare not take these promises to myself, it cannot be that this message of pardon is for me." Is not this thought the great stumbling-block in the way of all, when they are awakened and become concerned about their souls? This is our first lesson; and only when we have learned and believe, that our guilt is gone—washed away in the precious blood of Christ; that He is our propitiation, and that in Him we are justified and accepted—though our sins have been red as scarlet and crimson—though we know that we by nature and apart from Christ are in a just state of eternal condemnation: only when we have learned and believe this, only

then have we left the bondage of the law, and the fear of death, and entered the family of God as His forgiven, His beloved children in Christ! — You remember, in the Pilgrim's Progress, how Christian toiled along with his load on his back? Ah, as long as he walked oppressed with that, all was up-hill; desire, but not hope; resolves and legal fears, but no freedom, no power. But when he came to the cross and there knelt down, his burden fell off and was removed from that moment. "He has given me rest by His sorrow and life by his death!" So it is with all of us—the burden of guilt is entirely removed. Faith in Christ includes this. As long as a man struggles to free himself from it, so that he may be fit and worthy to come to Christ—struggle he never so hard and try every means: so long he has not the Gospel-faith and cannot enjoy the Gospel-peace! No, he must *assume* his pardon upon God's declaration, must forget his guilt as one of the things which are now behind him, or he has no peace and cannot run his course except oppressed by the curse. Like the prisoner whose pardon is sealed and whose bonds are knocked off, the poor sinner who has brought his guilt to Jesus and heard Him say, "Son, daughter, thy sins be forgiven thee," rises from the dust and leaps in the enjoyment of his freedom, and forgets his guilt as past; and if memory brings it up, it is only to raise his heart in gratitude to Him that saved him, and to devote himself, in a godly life and in the walk of that perfect liberty with which Christ has made him free, to His service and to His His glory. — "I will have mercy on their unrighteousness and their sins I will remember no more." Surely, brethren, if God forgets them, *may not we?*

Forgetting those things which are behind, among them are—

2. *Our sins.* This is more difficult, I admit. It is easier for a man to persuade himself that pardon is extended to him, than to feel the power of sin broken in his heart and life. Our sins assail us constantly and beset us on all sides, and as long as we live. But just on that account, brethren, I say, the rule of the Apostle is so all-important—forget them, try to forget them. Look not to yourselves, but look to Jesus and His promises, believe in His victorious power and engage in the active course of holiness and good works; and your attention may be drawn from them and you thus will be freed from their perilous influence. Their very remembrance has a pestiferous power; the very struggles to which you resort against them may rivet their image upon you, and thus perhaps their dangerous, engrossing power. It is one of the most humiliating experi-

ences we can make, that the devil often uses our very struggles as a means to continue in us the remembrance, and with it, to some extent, the fascination of the sin we have renounced. Let the man that had fallen a victim to sensuality be touched by the spirit of God and become a Christian: the devil, you may be sure, will not cease plying him with the images of his former lusts. And do you believe, that a course of fighting against these sins, which would constantly bring up their power and allurements and their polluting remembrance, will be apt to ensure success? Let a man even pray against them and think he strives against them in the strength of the Lord: I believe and I know that there may be danger even in this, and that the only course of safety is *in flight, in forgetting them and reaching forth to more profitable occupations of our thoughts and time.* — It is so with the reformed drunkard; it is so with every one that has lived in slavery to some darling sin; and well would it be for all of us to heed this lesson.

After all it is a form of self-righteousness to think *we* must renounce, *we* must resist, *we* must do the work of victory. No, beloved, it is more Christian and it is safer, to commit even our conflict with sin to the Lord; and believing, that He is willing and able to save us, not only from guilt but also from *sin*, its love and dominion—instead of seeking our religious life in this defensive warfare, to *go on in the positive course of Christian obedience, and forget our former sins in the absorbing thought of our present duties and privileges.* I cannot be of the opinion of those who—surely from very good motives and apparently with great plausibility, and from a high Christian stand-point—urge upon the sinner, in his prayers and self-examination to make special declaration to God of all his most heinous sins in thought, word, and deed. It seems to me they declare and demand only what *they think* a Christian *ought to* feel and do. They speak without any real experience, any deep and humbling experience; they do not speak of what they have seen and heard and felt, painfully, tearfully felt. I think Luther is right when, in opposition to this monkish kind of penance, he warns men against hazarding the pollution of their imagination by this recapitulation and renewing of sins and their images in detail. "Do not," he says, "stand picking the flaws out one by one, but plunge into the river and drown them!" Yes, I can assure you, brethren, that the only certain way of victory over our sins, is to cast aside the very remembrance of them, and by faith *assume* ourselves delivered from them; to *forget them* and even ask God in earnest, agonizing prayer never to let us think of them again; to forgive us if we even do no longer pray against that sin which so easily besets us, and often by its very remembrance overcomes us anew; ask Him to fill our mind with other things and, forgetting those things which, through faith in Him, we bury once for all, reach forth to better things before and engage actively in our new duties!

And as it is with sins, so with errors; the best way to free the mind from error is to fill it with truth. So it is with temptations. I know no other way to overcome them but to flee and plunge into some good, and godly, and sanctifying work. — So it is with our broken resolutions. Ah, brethren! go to God in the humbling sense that you have too often violated and broken your most solemn vows, and pray Him "who alone can order the unruly wills and affections of sinful men," to take you in hand, rather than let you guide yourselves; to make you all you ought to be, enable you to do all He wants you to do, and ever to live before Him with the prayer "Lord, what wilt Thou have me to do?"

Forgetting the things which are behind, among them finally are:—

3. *Our attainments!* and this indeed is one of the chief points the Apostle makes: "not as tho' I had already attained, either were already perfect." But is it necessary for me to dwell on this point now?

Can any be here present, whatever their course may be in practice, who in theory at least and open confession, would say that they can rest on their attainments, and thank God that they have advanced so well and made such good use of their opportunities, and lived so consistently and close to the cross? No, brethren, I would rather have you give your thoughts to the things we have just spoken of, and be deprived of the true liberty and highest energy of the Christian, than rest at ease in your profession and attainments. The first at least would humble you and perhaps lead you nearer the cross; the last would deaden all spiritual life, and finally identify your hope with that of the hypocrite. There is no rest for us in the pursuit of our calling. The field grows the more faithfully we work it. Its prospect extends, the higher we rise. And he has lost the spirit of Christ who can sit down at ease; who forgets that the true secret of Christian perfection is this: "forgetting all my attainments, and counting them but insufficient, and deriving nought from their remembrance but the trembling sense of insufficiency and the undying desire for more grace—I find my only safety and happiness in doing better than I have done in the past; in reaching forth to the things yet before me, to every time and every opportunity; and thus, in pressing forward towards the mark for the prize of the high calling of God in Christ Jesus."

Ah! here it is where we meet our deepest sorrows. How many Christians, how often do all of us, fall short in this particular; how many think so much of their attainments which are behind, that they have no time and no heart to think of a new and better course before them!

Beloved, the Christian's watchword is, *press towards the mark*. That mark is perfection! Have we reached it? His course, the very essence of his life, is *progress!* Can we look upon ourselves as Christians if we do not progress? I mean, if we are not striving to advance; for we cannot be satisfied with the progress we have made (take comfort in that thought, every earnest, mourning soul!) His great assurance is, that his high calling of God *is in Christ Jesus; not apart from Christ, nor beyond Him,* (that would be a hopeless calling,) but IN HIM, in whom is given us every promise of grace, sufficiency and everlasting blessedness! In Him, the power of hope, which maketh not ashamed. In Him that love which overcometh the world and triumphs over sin and death!

And if this is my calling, dare I lag behind? Brethren, dare I stay in condemnation when the spirit of Holiness is to change me into His own image from glory to glory? Dare I remain undecided and halt between two opinions when eternity is at stake, and Christ has bled for me and Christ ensures the victory? *Dare I remain as I am?* Oh! beloved, it is a blessed truth that we are bid to come "just as we are;" that Christ meets us in all our wretchedness; that He came into the world to save sinners. But, *dare we remain so?* I trust there is no egotism in it, but I believe you can scarcely find any one who is more urgent than myself in inviting you to come "just as you are," and pointing you to the full, unlimited, unconditional invitation to the worst of sinners. But have I ever told you, "*remain as you are?*"—Remain just as we are? Why, the very essence of the Gospel is this: That it changes us from sinners to saints, that Christ gave Himself for us, for this high and holy purpose, not to save sinners *in* their sins and carry them to heaven in their carnal mind and corruption, but to redeem them and purify them from all sin. *No, we go to Jesus just for these things.* Poor, wretched, blind, as we are, we come—but with the prayer:

> Sight, riches, healing of the mind;
> Yea, all I need in Thee to find!
> * * Thy love unknown
> Has broken every barrier down;
> Now to be Thine—

Thine, with all the desires of the heart, all the

affections of the soul, all the efforts of my strength, the powers and faculties of my mind! *Thine*, with all I am and have—

> Yea, Thine alone—
> Oh Lamb of God, I come!

And now I say behold the offers and the provisions of the Gospel! Are they not sufficient for all, for every want? There is the blood of Christ for your guilt—the power of His spirit and constraining love against the power and love of sin—the aggressive, onward life of holiness against our unprofitable attainments. *All is ready! Are you?*

To my unbelieving brethren I say, "this one thing do:" Forget the past with its sorrows and sins and foolish hopes. Your reaching forth is, to go to Jesus and count all things but loss to win Him and know Him, and the power of His resurrection. *Or* your reaching forth is into hell-fire; the mark towards which you are pressing the pillory of eternal damnation.

To the anxious enquirer, I say "this one thing do:" Go no longer about to establish your own righteousness, dwell no longer on the fears of the past and your own hopeless condition. Forget self, look unto Jesus, the author and finisher of our faith, and find peace and righteousness and strength in

Him who came to call sinners, not the righteous, to repentance.

But to the Christian I say, "press on, press towards the mark for the prize of the high calling of God in Christ Jesus"—

> Fight the fight, Christian,
>   Jesus is o'er thee!
> Run the race, Christian,
>   Heaven is before thee!
> Thee from the love of God
>   Nothing shall sever;
> Rise, when thy work is done,
>   Praise Him forever!

Which of you intending to build a tower sitteth not down first and counteth the cost, whether he have sufficient to finish it?

LUKE xiv. 28.

It hardly seems strange that this text should have been often used in justification of delay. "We must count the cost," and therefore "must not hurry into a profession of religion—must put it off until we are sure all is right and every doubt and difficulty removed." But, in reality, the Saviour's parabolic language only reproves a shallow, superficial religion, not an honest confession of Christ made at once. He never allows of delay. "Now is the time," the only time, as in all Scripture. "Seek ye first the kingdom of God" refers to religion, not only as the main thing in importance, but as the first in time. Whatever hinders or causes delay, is forbidden. "Let the dead bury their dead." — Christ did not reprove the multitudes for coming to Him, but for coming thoughtlessly and for the wrong thing—for the bread which perisheth, and not the bread of life. —

ETERNITY *is before you*, my brethren, with its tremendous issues—you cannot help that—*you must be Christians* or *you are lost!* that point is settled.

You must be so at once—no reprieve of a "to-morrow," no "convenient season." All our time is claimed by God. "Just as I am" is the confession, for no previous qualification affects it. "*Too late*" will be the sad and hopeless lesson if we do not learn "to-day," that we know not what "the morrow" may bring forth! Therefore lose no time, but at once choose that course which alone can secure salvation, choose it in earnest, and as reasonable, accountable beings—"the night is far spent, the day is at hand."

Christianity is the fairest of all systems. There is no disguise, no holding back with God, nor can such be with us in our relation to Him. People may attempt it with their fellow-creatures, may try to cheat themselves perhaps, but before God? "All things are naked and open unto the eyes of Him with whom we have to do."—

Thus God does not withhold from us the true issues of our immortal souls. He does not lure us into the church without telling us openly what is involved in it. He lays all before us, the *pros* and *cons*, and asks our intelligent and honest choice. And we, on our part, cannot pretend to enter His service and confess Christ with mental reservations, or hope to smuggle ourselves into the Kingdom of Heaven on false pretexts. There is no such thing as doing the work of the Lord deceitfully.

Brethren, like everything else, *religion costs something*. Our Saviour, so far from hiding this, speaks of going, if need be, against father and mother and every earthly tie and advantage, of cutting off the right hand and plucking out the right eye, rather than missing Heaven; aye, risking life itself, to save the immortal, never-dying soul.

It costs something to be a Christian, and we have to pay it!

Let us know exactly what it is, and see if we are able and willing to pay it; if, as it were, *we can afford it.*

I. Here, then, are the items on one side:

What we must pay and sacrifice.

1. *The pride of the heart.* — We love to think well of ourselves and feel elated, comparing ourselves with others that are less favoured by circumstances, or below us in attainments. A feeling of self-righteousness has been and is the natural desire of the human heart.

For what we call "the moral man," who prides himself on principle and self-control and character—it becomes a terrible struggle to come down, as he thinks, to the position of a poor, miserable sinner, who has to sue for pardon and renounce all hope in self and be saved only by grace! And yet, does not your conscience often whisper to you the truth, that all your claims are false, and that your life, without the grace of God, is a sham; at best, a shadow of better things to come?

Here is the difference between the open sinner and the moral man: The first has, indeed, the terrible drawback of vicious habits and a life-long bondage in sin and crime, but just on that account knows well enough there is no place for him but as a suppliant for mercy. But the difficulty of the man who thinks he is all right, to see and confess himself a helpless sinner! The blind eyes must first be opened, cleared to see both the perfect standard of God's holy law and his own short-comings; and the stiff heart must first break in the sense of unworthiness and ingratiude to the love that brings the sacrifice for his salvation, ere the choice can be made and the price paid down.

2. *The love of the heart*, its lusts and aspirations, the lust of the eye and the lust of the flesh, and the pride of life—and who does not know what this costs?

Resisting sin—which has grown up with us, grown with our growth and strengthened with our strength—which has gained the mastery over us by habit, which is more than what we call second nature, which is our *real nature*, so long as we remain in our unregenerate state, and which, in its countless forms and temptations, besets us as long as life lasts.

My dear brethren, if there was nothing but resisting sin, what would be our life? It would be a legal bondage all our days, a hopeless life-long struggle against what the Apostle calls "the condemnation of the law," for by the law is only the knowledge, not the cure, of sin.

3. *The sloth of the heart.*—Its love of ease and self-indulgence, the abjuring of it in the stern resolution of following after holiness, with sacrifices and self-denials to follow "whatsoever things are true, honest, just, pure, of good report, and do all to the glory of God!"

Ah! hard as that sounds, it is the very antidote of sin, the very power by which (with the help of God) we can overcome and rise to a new and better life—from slavery to freedom.

This statement, indeed, embraces all, but we may specify more minutely. Take the baptismal questions, ratified in confirmation—

1. Dost thou renounce the devil and all his works? Of course, I do!

Ah! but you don't know that if you do not serve Christ, you serve the devil! There is no neutral ground. And as little as the devil shows himself to you in his real form, so little does he approach you with the open demand "to fall down and worship him." He may come as an angel of light and beguile the soul with specious pretexts and deceitful hopes of light and power and knowledge. But whatsoever does not lead you to God and to His service through faith in Christ—call it self, or the world, or the prince of the world—it comes all to the same; it binds you to the apostate spirit, the adversary of God and man.

2. "The pomps and vanities of this wicked world." It is astonishing how different are the thoughts of God on this subject and the thoughts of man. In the Bible "the world, worldliness, worldly-mindedness," are represented as the very denial of godliness, the very essence of idolatry. With us—there is such a natural leaning towards it; we are ourselves so much influenced by its ways, which please the natural heart, that a pretended mantle of charity is cast over them as pardonable, natural foibles (very natural indeed!)

We speak of worldliness and conformity to worldly ways, and are answered: ah! but is not this a minor point? will you not allow different opinions? and where is the line of separation? Certainly, on single points, there may be and are differences, but not if principle is touched. And I believe more souls are ruined by the spirit of the world, by the hungering and thirsting after its honours, fashions, treasures, pleasures; by the slavish submission to its dictates, and temporizing with its overpowering influence, than by anything else. Oh! the toning down of religion and the standard of godliness! By profession Christ's peculiar people—and by everything else, just like all others in taste, desire, fashion, practice, in the broad road which can only lead to destruction!

Yes, peculiar! but why so peculiar and particular in little things? — May I not do *as others do?* — Would it be wrong *only once* to taste the forbidden fruit and to know the sin which I am to avoid? — Is there so much danger *once more* to touch it, to take, as it were, *a last farewell? How far* can I go without forfeiting my claim as a Christian? Is it wrong to do this or do that?—instead of asking: is it right, is it edifying, good for my growth in grace, a help to the Church, a glory to Christ? — And an impossible compromise is attempted!

3. "The sinful desires of the flesh."

Do not get angry with me, my brethren, if I say, with most of us more than the desires have to be renounced: the practice, the habit, open or secret! *Every sin* has to be given up, in the life, and even in the desire, in the heart, out of which are the issues of life. —

Are you ready to pay the price, to give up the darling sin which has enslaved you, to cut off what is dear to you as a right hand or a right eye, can you, will you *afford it?* Ah! I don't ask you to do it in your own strength. Are you willing to *endeavour to do it,* with the help of God and the all-sufficient grace of Christ? More cannot be asked, and that is all that is exacted of the candidate for baptism or confirmation.

Again: "Obey God's holy will and commandments," not some of them, but all; not now and then; not when you are baptized, confirmed, commune; not for a brief space of probation—but *all the days of your life.* Christianity is a very solemn thing, and Heaven a priceless possession.

Are you ready to work the works of God, to work in His vineyard now, and as long as He has need of you? Take His yoke upon you and learn of Him the lesson of obedience and unselfishness? be steadfast, unmoveable, always abounding in the work of the Lord? Are you ready to do this? *can you afford it?* Ah! not in your own strength; you are not asked to do that, but in the strength of Christ, who has promised His presence and sufficiency of grace. Are you prepared to run the race (to try it) which is set before you, with patience, looking unto Jesus, the author and finisher of our faith? To live by the prayer, "Lord, what wilt Thou have me to do?" and to press towards the mark for the prize of the high calling of God in Christ Jesus?

I am dealing openly with you, fairly. I dare not deceive you. Such are the issues.—It may be difficult, and but for the help vouchsafed and the platform of free grace and Christ's constraining love, it would be impossible.—It is difficult for flesh and blood. Even so! We do not deceive on that point. But, brethren, is it easy to learn Latin or Greek or French; to study mathematics or acquire skill in any art or occupation? And can we imagine it to be easier to learn the lesson of holiness and live as the children of God? There are temptations— many; but "no temptation shall befall you which is not common to man, and from which He will not make a way of escape;" the thorn in the flesh is there and will not necessarily be removed," but "His grace is sufficient for us."

The world's persecution and sneers? But Christ left the blessing "Blessed are they who are persecuted for righteousness' sake;" "Blessed are ye if men revile you and persecute you, and shall say all manner of evil against you falsely for My sake."

There is your business and its fancied importance, which hides the sight of God and eternity, and makes you grovel in the dust of earthliness; but Christ saith "one thing is needful."

My brethren, do you not see that these very difficulties, if you mean to be saved and choose life, make *immediate decision necessary for you?* Every moment of delay increases your danger, makes the difficulty greater, the sacrifices involved harder, the price more costly. — You say the world has claims on you. Certainly! But I say, only as Christians can you discharge your duty, be it in a private sphere or the public arena of life, "giving unto Cæsar the things which are Cæsar's, and unto God the things which are God's."

There is your family, your business, your friends, the laws of society, the fashion of the world. Very well! If you are Christians you will know how to serve God in all these, and how to behave yourselves, not only in the house of God, but as members of God's church in God's world, even His fallen world; and these very claims of life shall become means of grace to teach you, in its relative duties, to bring forth "fruits meet for repentance." But if they stand in your way to Christ, if you allow them to do so; that would be "loving father or mother more than Christ." You make them instruments of the devil, and must say "get thee behind me Satan, thou savourest not of the things of God, but the things of man."

You think religion offers you nothing but a joyless life of self-denial and sacrifice. Ah! I don't know. There are joys peculiar to the Christian, which eye hath not seen, ear hath not heard, nor the heart conceived. And I might say there is no higher life and greater bliss than self-sacrifice for a noble cause, than the loving service of God and His Christ. The service itself is its honour and its reward!

But suppose all you say is true. With your present taste you certainly deem it so. But the *fact* and the *necessity* remain the same. I cannot lower the terms of holiness. — *In one word:* are you ready to count all things but loss that ye may win Christ and know Him and the power of His resurrection? *Can you afford it?* Are you willing to pay it? *Say so now, for now is the time.*

II. I am sure you will allow I am honest in my statements. But now *per contra*.

I might point you to the provisions made for all these difficulties, in the free grace and the unfailing helps of the Gospel, and set off every self-denial and sacrifice with "the blessed hope set before us and the glorious appearing of our Lord and Saviour

Jesus Christ," at whose second coming we shall be found with Him in Glory. Aye, I might set them off with the blessedness of His love and presence *now*. The sufficiency of grace, the joy and peace He gives to the believer, the sure promises of the Gospel, not only of the life to come, but also of that which now is.

But you have been told that often, and you know it. Let me ask you, *can you afford to do without God* and without religion, without the atonement to be admitted into eternity and the presence of God, without the regenerating power of the Holy Ghost to become meet for heaven and eternal life?

You have immortal souls. Can you afford to give up eternity for the brief existence of threescore years and ten? Can you afford to risk eternal life for the pitiful gifts of this world, perishing, passing away like the world itself? "What shall it profit a man if he gain the whole world and lose his own soul?" Suppose you do gain all, would it be a resonable, profitable exchange? Would you be willing to stand by it in the last day, when Christ comes again and the judgment is set?

But look into real life. What does it give you? what do you get? At best only a larger amount of the essentials of life to which the greatest wealth at last reduces itself. "What shall we eat and what shall we drink, and wherewithal shall we be clothed?" A gilded form of what God, who feeds the fowls of the air and clothes the lilies of the field, gives to all His children; which, at best, is yours but for a few brief years on earth, but *with which* you have to take all its sorrows, trials, sufferings, and hopeless issues. Can you afford to make this your portion? — But more: Can you afford to give up every high aspiration—all the true glory of man? The purity of heart, without which you never can see God? The unselfishness, without which your heart can never be enlarged and taste of the powers of the world to come? The love, without which God's love is no blessing to you, and the soul which He made for Himself orphaned forever? The nobility, without which you cast away your highest glory and birthright—the image of God?

Are you ready to give up the hope of a godlike life, because you prefer the groveling pursuits and beggarly elements of this fleeting time and vanishing earth? Are you ready to say, "*World, thou art my God*, my rule, my joy, my portion, my all! and I seek not the favour of God, nor His kingdom and righteousness?" To un-soul yourself and live the animal? To un-man yourself and turn away from the bright hopes of humanity, and forswear that image of God in which man was first created, and which has been renewed in greater glory by the Incarnation and self-sacrifice of the Son of God, the second Adam? To be content to live a low, debased, degraded life, a life of sin that will revenge itself upon your soul, even here, and make you wretched in the contempt of self and the scorn of the world, and hurl you at last into a hopeless, dishonoured grave? Content to lead an unchristian life, "without God and without hope in the world?"

Oh! weigh these questions! Your character, your real being, your all for time and for eternity is involved in these questions and in their decision.

And consider: What is on the other side? The world cannot satisfy you, but Christ can! — There is pardon, acceptance, the citizenship of Heaven. There is comfort, peace, a good conscience. — There is a joyful looking forward to the rest that remaineth for the people of God. Endurance here of all the trials by the way, in patient waiting and faith. Power to live a godly and thus alone a truly human life, and fulfil your every duty, and shed blessings around you, benefit your fellow-men and reap their love and respect. Blessings amidst the sorrows and tears and persecutions of the world, and even the dark hours of Christian discipline: the favour of God which is life, and His loving kindness which is better than life.

Strike the balances, and say: *which* will you choose, *which can you afford?*

III. Once more: *Count the cost.*

Ah! you are not the only ones that have paid! *God himself has paid for your salvation!* He gave His Son!

Christ has paid to purchase eternal redemption, paid in that blood which cleanseth from all sin, but cries vengeance upon every soul that despises and rejects it. Dare you reject that? Can you afford to say "His blood be upon us and our children?"

I now ask, what is your verdict?

The love of God—this passing world?

Eternal life—a few moments of deceitful, disappointing hopes?

A high and holy nature—a nature depraved; corrupt, lost in the everlasting bondage to evil?

SALVATION or DAMNATION—WHICH CAN YOU AFFORD?

We are saved by hope.

Romans viii. 24.

Some men are saved by hope, and some men are lost by hope. Brethren, it is not mine to know the secrets of God's election, and the proportion of the redeemed and the finally doomed, nor to say if more are lost by hope or more are saved. But of this I am very confident, that of those who are lost most, nearly all, are lost by hope!

It is an awful thought: "Lost by hope!" Hope which, with its genial glow irradiates the darkness of this fallen world, and with its life-giving breath revives the dead and the despairing! Hope, the gracious boon of God's love when His justice had entailed the curse upon our race; which sweetened the labour of Adam and turned it into a blessing; which alone calls forth all the powers of the mind, and matures and developes the affections of the heart, so as to reclaim it from sinfulness and win it back to holiness and peace. Hope, the universal balm for the ills of life: There is no heart so desolate but it hears the voice of hope, no abode so dreary but it is visited by hope, no sigh so heavy but hope can lift it, no grief so deep but hope can smile through its tears.

Hope! which quickens the faith of the Christian and strengthens his endurance; which casts its glance into the future and sends the soul within the veil, through its uplifted eyes into the distant home, and clasps its hands in devout gratitude for that glory and that blessedness which are beckoning it to its eternal reward. Yes, Hope! the brighest, surest, most-abiding angel ministering to us on earth, raising the guilty heart and drawing its affections heavenward. Can it, can it be true, that by it souls are lost?

"Lost by hope!" I can understand how people may be lost by a fatal error in the grounds and subjects of hope. Sad experience and actual trial have taught us all to consent, in theory at least, to the truth, that "the hope of the hypocrite shall perish," that "he that trusteth in his own heart is a fool," that the self-righteous is "ignorant of the saving righteousness of God;" that the ceremonies and ordinances of the church cannot bring us to God unless we draw nigh to Him with the heart. There is but one hope which is good, which builds upon the rock everlasting; the hope in Christ, the good hope through grace.

"Lost by hope!" I can understand how a man may be lost in spite of every invitation and encouragement of hope, that speaks to him of heaven and salvation, or warns him with the dread alternative of hell and damnation; how he may be so engrossed in the enjoyment and the pursuit of earthly goods as to lose all ability to respond to the appeals that come to him from the invisible heights of the future, and give up all desire for peace and rest and happiness above and beyond the narrow circle in which he circumscribes his being; how he may be so much enslaved by the world, its joys and its cares, as to neglect both the promises and the warnings, and to live and die like the brute, without casting one thought, one sigh, one wish towards a better and a higher world.

But to be "lost by hope," *i. e.*, by the act of hoping, by the exercise itself of this faculty which leads him to realize the future issues of our life, and makes him live in the anticipation of that salvation which stands before him as the goal of his existence? — And yet, beloved, the painful truth is that the ruin of most souls is brought about, not so much by errors in doctrine, which make them cling to false grounds of hope, or by the want of aspiration for that immortality and blessedness which the human heart all but instinctively craves. You admit the truth of the Bible and the necessity of obeying its call; you acknowledge the claims of another world, and would not be without its blessed prospect for all this world could offer you. You hope, but, alas! to how many among us may that hope prove a savour of death? How many are there now, how many shall there be, when time is over in the realms of despair, who shall vainly cry and protest, "*We had hoped!*"—

There is a hope which appreciates the saving power of Christ and the reality of His redemption, and, therefore, rests on it and by faith rivets itself to Him and takes possession of His promises; climbs round after round the "santa scala" on which the penitent soul ascends from Calvary to the empyrean of God's presence; and all who thus hope are "saved by hope."

There is a hope which admits the saving power of Christ and the reality of His redemption, and, therefore, *looks forward* to the time when it, too, *shall* rest on Him, and resolves, *at some future day*, to seize its promises and accept its invitation. And all who thus hope are, to say the least, in danger of being "lost by hope." As long as they continue in this hope for a *future* interest in Christ, and speak peace to their hearts by the resolution *hereafter* to make their peace with God, and evade the appeal and call of Christ's minister by putting him off to some convenient season; so long they are in an actual state of condemnation, and this very hope but insures their final loss. All must be lost by their hope, who thereby are encouraged to put off the work of religion, were it only from day to day.

And now, my brethren, is not this the condition of almost every impenitent soul before me? You admit the truth of Christianity and the imperative character of its precepts, but you encourage yourselves in disobedience *by the hope of a future repentance.* There are none before me, I feel very certain—there are scarcely any anywhere—who say "I intend to live and die in my sins and never mean to be a Christian." Oh, no! all protest that they hope to be Christians and obtain salvation, but they ruin all by not being Christians *now*, by not coming to Christ now when He calls, now that life is theirs, now in the accepted time, the day of salvation.

I say, they ruin everything. For, brethren, cherishing this foolish hope of a future repentance, a future day when to seek and secure and profess an interest in Christ—why, for the present, they are doing nothing to bring it about; they have fixed their religious life at some indefinite future day, and in the meantime they live on just as they have lived; *i. e.*, as lost, hell-doomed, perishing, worldly, Christless sinners! And more, the very prospect of a future religious life, which they have in view, and which they know involves the renunciation of all their sins, perhaps makes them turn with the greater zest and eagerness to the indulgence for a season of those pleasures and practices of which that dreaded future day of religion, for such it becomes in their eyes, is to deprive them; and thus they may go on sinning worse and worse and becoming more and more unable to renounce it. And then, do you think they'll find it easier than now? Then, when the chains of their bondage are riveted faster around their unholy souls, when the continued practice of sin has driven out more and more the very desire for that change which now, at least, they can hope for; then they'll be prepared to do with ease and readiness, that which now they find so difficult—give up sin and live unto God, and come to Jesus. Ah! then that future day will be put off and put off till its very remembrance fades away from the mind, and it is adjourned indefinitely and quietly dropped; and vainly, vainly recalled, when they themselves shall drop into the grave and adjourn to another world! Can inconsistency, can perverseness, go farther?

All things are ready on the part of God. He is ready to pardon you, the Saviour is ready to sprinkle you with the blood of cleansing, the Holy Spirit is ready to purify and new-create your hearts, God's Word lies opon before you and shows the way so plain that the wayfaring man, though a fool, need not err therein; the herald of the cross even now calls upon you to turn and live! You, you alone, are not ready. The day of decision is ready; for let that great assize of the universe be as far off as it is possible for the human mind to form a conception of an interminable length of time, the question is settled at the moment of death—judgment is ready, the impenitent "condemned already," the believer saved "now!" Heaven is ready; its kingdom is within you. Hell is ready; the awful pit, on whose slippery brink you stand, is ready to swallow you up. *But you are not ready!* Not ready to be rescued from that perilous spot, though the hand of Infinite Mercy is stretched out for your salvation! Not ready? when nothing is required of you but to trust yourself to the pardoning and sanctifying power of Christ? Not ready? when no preparation is asked at your hands but to resolve, from this day onward, to try, by divine grace, to do better and obey God's will? Not ready? when every supply of help and every power necessary for your success is promised you in Christ, and when no length of time and no amount of effort on your part can bring you relief and help, until you have first gone to Christ, who alone can prepare you for heaven?

Yes! But you cannot make a profession of religion before you repent. And who asks you to make that profession without repentance? Repentance is its very essence; *i. e.*, turning from your sins to live unto God, and this we bid you do through faith in Christ. But you cannot profess Him without faith. And who asks you to do that? We bid you come to Jesus now, just as you are. You never can come otherwise than as sinners to be both pardoned and sanctified by Him; and this coming to Jesus, this flight of the soul from its state of condemnation and corruption into His saving arms, is Faith.

You say you hope to repent, you hope to exercise faith? What are you doing in the mean time? If you are putting off the question of religion, is that the way to get repentance? If you immerse yourselves anew in the cares and occupations of the world, and shut out God from your sight, thinking to come to Him hereafter; if you identify all your interests with this world, postponing for future consideration every claim of God and His Christ, is that the way to have your faith called forth and strengthened? Brethren, He that wills the end also wills the means!

But ah! may I not tell you, that in your best excuses you are not quite sincere! That it is, after all, your unwillingness to be Christians *now*, which keeps you from Him—not your want of preparation? There is but one way to solve the question, but one way to escape from the labyrinth of your numberless doubts and fears and drawbacks, your miserable little excuses by which, now this point now that, now a most tender regard for your own consistency, now the sneers and remarks of the world around you, are put up as pretexts. The only way to escape from all this is just to go to Jesus, just to cry " Lord, save or I perish," " Lord I believe, help Thou mine unbelief," " Lord, be merciful to me a sinner," " Lord, remember me," " Lord, make me a clean heart and renew a right spirit within me!"—

" Lost by hope!" You hope for a future day of God's power. That day is nowhere promised, but the day and the moment of promise is *the present!* And all experience proves, your own experience will tell you, the longer you put it off the harder the struggle will be, the more hopeless your case! It is not the aged nor those who, year after year, have sat under the preaching of the gospel and heard its calls and reproofs, and heard them in vain, that we can have much hope of. All they can do is to resolve and act *at once*, ere the last chance is gone and " the door shut." But ah! who, even of the youngest, has either the days of his life or the days of his grace in his power?

You hope for your passions to be cooled, for your state of mind to be better, for your strength to be greater to resist sin, for your preparation to be finished, for your hope to be confirmed that you will not sin again and bring discredit on your profession? No such hope leads to life! One passion may pass away—property, business, pleasure; and another starts up and clings even to the old man as he stoops to the grave. If you stay away from Christ and the means of grace you cannot gather strength, you cannot hope to walk as a child of God; and the longer you put off the work of religion for such reasons, the more your heart will be alienated from Him, the less able you will be to turn to Him and surrender to His saving grace.

Oh, ye the young! there is nothing more beautiful than to see the young man or maiden start on their course of life in the strength of the Lord God; nothing more sure of success than to have the Lord for your God and help—but oh! to see them harden their hearts, now so impressible; to see them go forth into the dangers of this life without the arm of Christ to lean on, without the restraints of His fear upon them! It all but ensures their ruin! And that very hope by which they put off the work of religion now, is but the weapon of the adversary to make their ruin more certain. If not now, when will you seek the Lord? when can you hope to find Him? Not till HE finds you on *the day of judgment!*

You hope in the mercy of God? That mercy is extended to you *now*, and pleads with you in accents of love and by tokens of affection, the neglect of which must increase your guilt and condemnation. His voice goes forth to you this day. Can you resist it? If so, will it not sound more faintly to-morrow, or next year; and perhaps lose its power upon you entirely! Have you never heard that Scripture "My spirit shall not always strive with man?"

Beloved, you may rest assured, that I am the last person in the world to cut off any one from true, evangelical hope. Myself a sinner and in daily need of forgiveness and hourly supplies of grace, I know how precious, I know how gracious and free it is. And with the full knowledge of this truth of God, and with the solemn sense of my responsibility, feeling how the blood of your souls will be required of me if I teach you falsely, I affectionately and authoritatively extend to all, the best and the worst among you alike, those who think themselves strongest and those who think themselves weakest alike, those who have profited most and those who thus far have profited least by the teaching of God, I offer to all the invitation of my Master and bid them "come to Him," and now, this day, rest your hope in Him! And I say, it is a good hope, that shall not make you ashamed!

But to put off! to hope for a future day? to say to Christ, "Go Thy way—not to-day," to wait even for the morrow—oh! it involves dangers which I fear to contemplate. There is no promise for the morrow in the Bible. Hope, true hope, fades for all who turn from God now. I only know that *this* is the day of salvation, *this* the accepted time; but that he who trusts in a future day may pass the bounds of grace, may be lost eternally, lost by his false hope " Ephraim joined to his idols, and God saying, ' Let him alone!'"

> There is a time, we know not when,
>   A point, we know not where,
> That marks the destiny of men—
>   To glory or despair.
>
> There is a line, by us unseen,
>   That crosses every path;
> The hidden boundary between
>   God's patience and His wrath.
>
> To pass that limit is to die—
>   To die, as if by stealth.
> It does not quench the beaming eye,
>   Or pale the glow of health.

The conscience may be still at ease,
    The spirits light and gay;
That which is pleasing still may please,
    And care be thrust away.

But on that forehead God has set,
    Indelibly, a mark;
Unseen by man, for man, as yet,
    Is blind and in the dark.

And yet the doomed man's path below
    May bloom, as Eden bloomed;
He did not, does not, will not know,
    Or feel, that he is doomed.

He knows, he feels that all is well,
    And every fear is calmed;
He lives, he dies,—he wakes in hell!
    Not only doomed, but damned!

Oh! where is this mysterious bourne,
    By which our path is crossed?
Beyond which God himself has sworn
    That he who goes is lost?

How far may we go on in sin?
    How long will God forbear?
Where does Hope end, and where begin
    The confines of despair?

An answer from the skies is sent:
    "Ye that from God depart,
While it is called 'to-day repent',
    And harden not your heart."

Having, therefore, these promises, dearly beloved, let us cleanse ourselves from all filthiness of the flesh and Spirit, perfecting holiness in the fear of God.

II. CORINTHIANS vii. 1.

The religion of our Lord and Saviour Jesus Christ acts upon His followers in a two-fold manner. It *puts them* in a state of safety and everlasting happiness, for "there is no condemnation to them that are in Christ Jesus;" and *it puts upon them* a holy and divine character, for "they walk not after the flesh, but after the spirit." This condition and this character of the Christian always go hand in hand.

The object of the wondrous grace of God is certainly the happiness of our poor fallen race; but only as it is connected with its *holiness*. God would never have sent His Son into the world to save beings that would continue unholy. Only in this connection both the purposes of God and the interests of man can stand. The happiness of beings changed from sinners to saints, the new creation of the power of His holiness, is the highest glory of God which is revealed to men and angels. The holiness which is engendered in the heart of man by the promise of such happiness and the knowledge of the love which brought it to him, is the highest element in his happiness.

The promise comes *from above;* the happy state of salvation and immortal blessedness in the reconciliation of God, is prepared *for us from without* by another, even our Saviour. *The holiness* which forms the character of those who are endowed by His grace with this happiness, is *developed from within*, in the heart of man, by the powerful agency of the Spirit of holiness.

The great thing, then, for men to do is,—resting on the promises of God and believing in the power of the Saviour—to purify themselves as He is pure, to learn of Jesus, who gives them rest, and strive to be like Him. This is "being a Christian!"

Let us cleanse ourselves from all filthiness. Here we learn, first, that the earliest work of the Christtian (and, alas, owing to our defiled nature, the strength of sin, the weak hold of all that is good and holy, the powerful hold and influence of the world, which lieth in evil, it continues his work unto the end of this life below) is *a conflict with evil, a renunciation of sin, a process of purification.* And by this very confession, by the vow we take when entering Christ's Church, "to renounce the world, the flesh and the devil," we acknowledge our sinful nature, and our state of condemnation and corruption, out of which we are delivered by the grace of God.

And, secondly, we learn how *broad* the commandments of God are, how *thorough* must be the Christian's work: from *all filthiness*, from *all and every sin!* Herein the Christian scheme differs so essentially from all the various schemes of reformation which have been pressed upon us. It alone makes of man a new creature! It sets him against *all* sins, not this or that one which may be so glaring and so destructive to worldly success and respectability among men, that in their renunciation God need not have any share or glory. *It knows no sin which its disciple dare indulge in.* He who is a Christian at all, fears God and knows that he breaks the whole law if he offends in one point. He knows no venial sins, no indulgences which he may adopt by way of compensation for others which he denies himself. His law forbids every sin; and more—it leads him to contend against sinfulness, against the evil that is *within*, against the corrupt bias of the heart. He must not only regard the whole *breadth* of God's commandments, but he must go *the full length of it;* pursue sin beyond and beneath its outward phenomena and attack it in the heart. He cleanses himself from all filthiness *not only of the flesh, but also of the spirit.* It is the *motive* which, after all, qualifies the act; and the Christian must clear that, clear the ground, tear up the evil root, and not be satisfied with mere pruning. *In the heart* lust is conceived; there he attacks it and conquers it, and there, too, prevents its bringing forth sin; *in the heart* it is that covetousness sets up its idols, and there the Christian must defeat it. And it is this searching character of his holiness which unmasks many an act which the world might praise; his prayers, his charitable deeds, his self-denials—*all* are weighed in the spiritual balance of the law of Jesus and found wanting, if the principle is wrong. And in the heart and spirit he discovers sins which the world scarcely knows or frowns upon; pride, self-love, unbelief, and everything that exalts man and puts down God and His Christ!

Oh, my brethren, is it wonderful that the Christian should have such a deep sense of human depravity, when he has learned it by searching his own heart according to such rules? And can we look upon those who, against the testimony of God, exalt the grandeur of the human soul and deny the deceitfulness and desperate wickedness of the heart, otherwise than as guilty of using a false balance and deceitful weights? If you want to know the Christian try him on these points. Try yourselves, brethren, before God and your conscience. If you are at ease in your own mind, careless as to sin or duty, without a deep sense of your sinfulness, you have not striven as you ought to do, to cleanse yourselves from all filthiness of the flesh and spirit. For all those who have not learned to condemn themselves, have neither learned to know God's law nor themselves! — And nothing makes the Christian walk more warily and circumspectly; nothing keeps him closer to Jesus, and more fearful of temptation and even the appearance of evil; nothing, therefore, frees him more from these very abominations, and from everything that God looks upon as filthiness; nothing makes his character shine brighter and qualifies him better for the highest attainments of godliness, than this humbling conviction of his own sinfulness and weakness, which makes him kneel at the foot of the cross and pray "make me a clean heart, and renew a right spirit within me." And nothing, surely, can raise his love to Jesus higher, than the consciousness of all the innumerable sins which only His love that passeth understanding could forgive, "for to whom much is forgiven, the same loveth much."

But more; the Christian's virtue is *not merely negative*. It does not consist in only abstaining from sin. *It perfects holiness.* It goes out after everything that is true and honest and just and pure and lovely and of good report. It follows the example of the Master and "goes about doing good;" it searches out ways and means to glorify the Saviour and adorn His profession with all the Christian graces, and become as "a burning and shining light," to His praise and glory. Its aim is ever *onward; perfection, and nothing but perfection* satisfies him, for all else falls short of the glory of God. He rests in His faith indeed, and fears no storm that could move him from the Rock of Ages. And though his horizon be dark and his own corruptions make him weep and mourn, he still lights up his darkness with the undying flame of faith and hope. But his faith is not alone; it has creative energy and is surrounded by all the graces of the Gospel "love, joy, peace, long suffering, gentleness, goodness, meekness, temperance." In them he follows the bright example which Christ left His disciples; and the Christian, who is "God's workmanship, created *in* Christ Jesus *unto* good works," grows unto the perfect man, "unto the measure of the stature of the fulness of Christ." Thus he perfects holiness in the fear of God. In the fear of God, brethren! *This is the principle* which distinguishes all, even his least important acts, from those of others, they are all "*begun, continued and ended in God,*" and thus only are they *truly Christian acts;* thus only sufficiently guarded against every temptation and every evil; thus only sufficiently supplied with needful strength and light, and thus only the Christian is enabled to fulfil the great commandment of God, to seek *that holiness which is unto the Lord.*

I have thus, very feebly, drawn the outlines of the aims, the strivings, the whole character of the Christian; that holiness which distinguishes him from all others. Deficient as the image is, I yet boldly ask: show me one in all the history of the world, in all the products of imagination, in all the dreams of philosophy, that can compare with it. Aye, Brethren, even if Christianity were what its enemies would fain make it out to be, a mere fable, a fond delusion; if that fable is able to bring about such results, and educate such characters, the like of which nothing else has ever produced; if that delusion furnishes the world with the only specimen of perfect truth and highest virtue; if it converts and has converted millions from profane, idle, debauched lives, into sober, righteous and godly men; if it has furnished a code of morality, in comparison with which the highest productions of Greek or any other philosophers are abominations, and not only furnished the code but illustrated it by living examples; and if, as all history proves, whatever is great and glorious has been fostered by it, and the noblest, the highest, the most intellectual, and most permanently useful men that ever adorned our race, have formed a halo round her crown which sheds a brighter light upon the annals of humanity than all else; then I still, and every rational being still, would rather follow *this fable*, than all the inefficient and effete abortions of a high sounding, but in comparison with it, not only a *low-born* but a *low-keeping* philosophy, or all the scurrilous impostures which have made fools of those who deemed themselves too wise to believe the Bible.

Yes, *the moral results of Christianity* are perhaps the strongest proof of its divinity. There is no enthusiasm or fanaticism here, no temporary success, but *a settled principle* that has been victorious at all times and among all nations and classes of men. A principle with which none but the libertine, none but those who are willing to boast of their shame can find fault; a universal fitness, even in its language, in all its sentiments, in every reproof, in every promise, which has never left an inquirer without an answer, and a penitent without comfort; and a life-giving power which has lined the canvass of this world's tableau with a shining train of saints, from its founder down to the humblest Christian in this house, before which all other glories of this world fade away. If this institution were not divine, if its author were not God, surely old Gamaliel's saying was full of wisdom—it would have come to nought. But as it is of God it cannot be overthrown; the gates of hell itself shall not prevail against it. And has it ever struck you that nothing ever has opposed it but what comes from hell or goes there? *Beware!*

But the great question for us, my brethren, to decide is this: Can we claim for ourselves this character of holiness which has been shown to be inseparable from the state of salvation into which Christianity puts its votaries? Let each one ask, *Am I thus holy?* And is there one who does not bow his head in sorrow and confusion, and smite upon his breast and say, "God be merciful to me, a sinner!"

My dear Christian brethren, if it was necessary for the Christian to boast that he had already attained, either were already perfect, what hope would there be for us? No, thank God, the Christian stands in the righteousness of Christ and not his own; and Paul himself has taught us to distinguish between attainments and aims or aspirations "not as though I had already attained, but I press towards the mark!" No true Christian ever boasted of his attainments, but *all true Christians aim at nothing less than perfection.*

The demands of God's law we cannot lower. Whether you are Christians or not, professors of religion or not, *they will be made on you.* Whether there be a Christ or no, you must—if you do not mean to remain as you are "condemned already," to remain dead here and in all eternity—you must cleanse yourselves from all filthiness of the flesh and spirit, and live unto the Lord, "perfecting holiness in the fear of God." This *must* be your aim if you mean to have *any hopes* at all, whatever your premises be.

But behold how large and how gracious the offer which is made us, which is made to all, just in this Gospel which we preach, just in the revelation which takes the high ground we have laid down.

There is full, plenary forgiveness promised and ensured to all who will accept Jesus as their Saviour. There are none who do not come under its provisions; none who are at heart worse; none, I dare say, who are worse in their lives than some of those were who have availed themselves of the invitation and laid hold by faith on the promises set before us. "Though your sins be as scarlet and red like crimson, they shall be as white as snow and as wool." What Christian is there who does not confess, that if it was not for this promise there would be no hope for him? Are your sins, my impenitent brethren, worse than these and of a deeper dye than scarlet and crimson? Oh! look upon your Saviour! look upon Jesus, who, from the cross where He died for you, prayed for your forgiveness, and has said to all "Come unto Me and be ye saved, all the ends of the world!" Look upon Him and take *His* salvation, for whose sake alone all who ever have gone or shall go to heaven have been pardoned and blessed with an everlasting salvation. You are just bid to throw your sins upon *Him*, and thus freed from their burden and their guilt, accepted *in His name* by God, who will welcome you as beloved children: *to resolve*, under the influence of that same grace which offers you life eternal, to devote yourselves to a new and better life; "to renounce all filthiness of the flesh and the spirit and strive to perfect holiness, in the fear of God." This is *all!* ALL! And is it possible that men will refuse? That you, my dear, my beloved brethren, for whose souls Christ died, to whom heaven has been opened by His death and passion; for whose salvation your pastors, your friends, the whole Church of God bow their knees and offer up their warmest prayers—that you will refuse the salvation offered? Look upon those promises, survey those blessings!

There is God the Father waiting to be gracious. There is Christ, the beloved, who underwent all that suffering for you and now beseeches you to let Him save you, and present you, holy and blameless, to *His* and your Father! There is the Holy Spirit who has been wrestling with you long and not yet withdrawn, and urges you on the way to holiness and bliss, and woos you to the abode of safety, who engages to help and guide you and to beat down Satan under your feet! Heaven, from one end to the other, is in league with you and interested in your victory, and its holy angels are waiting to welcome you and to rejoice over every sinner that repenteth! There are the millions saved by the same salvation which is offered to you, a cloud of witnesses to the blood and spirit of Jesus, to cheer you on and meet you in the blessed mansions— perhaps an honored father, a loving mother, who even in heaven remembers her prodigal child; a son or daughter gone before, and now whispering to you in the stilly night when your evil conscience beds you on a restless couch, and speaking heavenly words to you in dreams, and saying "Come!" There are friends, and brothers and sisters, wives and husbands, who never say a prayer, but your soul is prayed for; who never look you in the face but to watch the signs of quickening grace! *And more!* there is the promise of help, the promise of sufficiency, of strength according to your days, the promise that no temptation shall befall you from which God will not deliver you; that all things shall work together for your good; the promise that

> "The soul that to Jesus has fled for repose,
> He will not, He will not desert to His foes;
> That soul, though all hell should endeavour to shake,
> He'll never, no never, no never forsake!"

Oh! my impenitent brethren! you who have resisted so many calls, what can I say to you? Do you not feel, do you not know, that we are right and you are wrong? That we urge you to the only course of safety, whilst you are in the straight road to perdition? Do you not know and feel, that *this life* in which alone you can escape and make your calling and election sure *is short, is uncertain?* What security have you that another day will be allowed you in which to make your peace with God?

> Lo! on a narrow neck of land
> 'Twixt two unbounded seas you stand:
> Yet how insensible!
> A point of time, a moment's space
> Removes you—*where?*
> WHERE?

Oh! that I could burn this question into your

souls: "Where?" That it might accompany you wherever you go, and force itself upon your attention every hour and moment of your lives, in every company, at every occupation, and haunt you with its import, till you have sought the peace which alone can give you rest!

Do you not know and do you not feel that an eternity is before you, an eternity of woe or bliss, and that its issues depend *on your choice here?*

> Oh think, when heaven and earth are fled
>   And times and seasons o'er,
> When all that can die shall be dead,
>   That *you* shall die no more.
> Oh where will then your portion be,
> *Where* will you spend eternity?

Where? WHERE? Oh, that I had a thousand tongues to haunt you with this question, and let it sound and resound in your ears, when my voice has died away—"where?"

Thank God, you still have space and time for repentance. Once more you are privileged to hear the Gospel, once more you are called upon to make your choice.

And now in the name of God Almighty, I lay this claim before you; and ere you cross this threshold, ere you add once more the sin of receiving Christ's grace in vain to your long, long disobedience to his call of love, I tell you *choose*. By all the authority of God, by all the love of Jesus, by the hopes and fears of your immortal soul, *choose!*

You cannot leave this house without receiving or rejecting Christ in your heart. You cannot leave this house without choosing whom you will serve.

Mark the alternatives, and may God guide you in your choice; I shall remind you of it in the other world: that you cannot go from these sacred precincts to-night without one of these alternatives. No other issue is possible.

You either resolve,

"God, I will give Thee my heart, Jesus, I accept Thy promises, and with Thy grace assisting me, I will cleanse myself from all filthiness of the flesh and spirit and perfect holiness in the fear of God."

Or,

"God I defy Thee, Jesus I spurn Thy promises, and I will not cleanse myself from all filthiness of the flesh and spirit. I will not perfect holiness in the fear of God."

And can you blame the Gospel, if of such it saith. "these shall go into everlasting punishment, but the righteous into life eternal."

I am Thine—save me.

Ps. 119, 94.

Work out your own salvation!

Phil. ii. 12.

"Lord, I am Thine, save me!" is the cry which ascends from the deep heart of the Psalmist to the throne of grace of God in heaven. — It is a wonderful prayer! It involves the most blessed assurance of perfect security, "Lord, I am Thine;" and yet, with it all goes the wrestling, agonizing cry "save me!" The complete rest of the soul in Christ, the rock of ages; but with it, the ever-realized necessity of the soul, with the saving help of God still to make its calling and election sure.

The two ideas run parallel through all scripture. "Believe in the Lord Jesus Christ and thou shalt be saved" indeed embodies both. — My brethren, if you had your Bibles with you, I could lead you from text to text to prove that that belief, and that belief *only*, involves *a present salvation;* and there is *no future salvation which does not begin in the present.* " He that hath the Son " (believeth on Him) hath, *h-a-t-h* life—*not shall have!* And from the same Bible I could confirm the words of my other text, "Work out your own salvation;" "Present your bodies a living sacrifice, holy and acceptable unto God;" "Strive to enter in;" "Press toward the mark;" "Wage a good warfare;" "Be thou faithful unto death, and I will give thee a crown of life!"

Now, is not this a most important, is it not the vital question for the Christian? *What is the relation of the two? God's work and our work?* Where does grace end and work begin? or, *vice versa*, work end and grace begin? The line is invisible; for in one aspect all is of grace, beginning, middle and end—the willing and the doing; in another all points to our work—even the response to the call, the acceptance of the grace.

But we must distinguish.

1. It is not ours *to work*, *i. e.*, to make, create, procure our salvation. There is no salvation unless it is free—"without money," "without price," without our working for it. That would be no gospel, but a mockery—a hopeless impossibility! Salvation *begins* in our taking the free salvation offered in the gospel; in taking Christ, who came into the world to save the helpless, hopeless sinner! "Lord, I am Thine! By Thine own act of redemption in Christ! I take Thee as my Saviour, and now stand in Thy righteousness and power, not my own: *I am Thine!*"

Faith appropriates Him. "With the heart man believeth unto righteousness." And beloved there is no life, no beginning, no hope, no place to stand on, but this grace of God, this God-thought, God-word, God-work of redeeming love, which precedes all that we can think or say or do. Nothing but the merits and the work and love of Christ, and the Father's adoption of the sinner in Him! We have just to give up! to knock under, (if I may use the expression,) and as poor, helpless, guilty sinners, that can bring no ransom, and work out no cancelling and supererogatory merit, to receive God's pardon and acceptance in Christ and say, " Lord, I am Thine!"

Birth before growth, life before work, pardon before payment, acceptance before merit, adoption before meetness. *That is God's way!* There is no grace without it! Salvation of the guilty sinner can only be of grace. Accepting that grace makes us God's!

I cannot delay to argue that point to-day. The denial of it is the denial of God's truth all through, that unbelief which at last is the only "damning" and "damnable" sin, for it keeps us from Christ who alone can save from sin, its guilt and power, and His blood which "cleanseth from all sin!"

No salvation out of Christ! No salvation possible!

Sin unpardoned, guilt unforgiven, without faith in Christ, without the abjuring of all hope in self, and *resting for all and resting only on Christ!* Oh! the fearful perversion of the human mind, not to see the freeness of God's salvation, not to learn that there is but one way for the sinner to come—

> "Just as I am," without one plea,
> But that Thy blood was shed for me,
> And that Thou bidst me come to Thee!

Those miserable excuses "I am not good enough." Did Christ come into the world to save the good or to save sinners? "I must first be strong enough before I can commit myself to Christ!" And can there be strength before you have Christ, to grow strong in Him? "Finally, my brethren," writes the Apostle, "be strong in the Lord and in the power of His might!" Can you do that, have that, unless you first are the Lord's? give yourselves to Him as sinners in all your weakness? What saith the same apostle? "When I am weak then I am strong—strong in the Lord." "Every doubt solved?" Who can do that but Christ? And He will not solve any doubts which do not touch the real point. How ridiculous to speculate about doctrinal propositions and dogmatic systems, and forget your soul's immediate wants: Eternal life, man's sin, God's holiness and mercy, and the counsel of grace that alone harmonizes all? Christ received in your heart as your Saviour and your King? —

And, brethren, are not most doubts of *a moral nature?* I mean, arising from moral difficulties in your way, and perhaps immoral tendencies and practices begotten in the love of the world, its fashions and sins, that your conscience tells you are so hard to harmonize, impossible to harmonize with God's law "without holiness no one shall see the Lord!" That holiness can be obtained only in Christ and by giving up all else.

But again, and oh, the many who come to us with that trouble—"my Christianity is so imperfect." Why of course it is—and I know it to be much worse than you think it—I know it by my own experience. But *your Christianity?* is that to save you? your poor, miserable, inconsistent, worldly Christianity? the consciousness of which should indeed make you penitent? But is that to keep you from Christ? Who, *what* saves you? your own Christianity or *Christ?* The poorer your Christianity, the more you need Christ—and, as if you had never known Him before, you should now go to Him and count all your past but loss, and lay hold of Him now as your only salvation!

Do not deceive yourselves! If you want to be a better Christian go at once to Christ. Plant yourself upon His merits—plead His love and the Father's love, who is no hard Master, and say, "Lord, whatever the past has been (ah, it has taught me my weakness and the strength of sin upon me) Lord Jesus, *yet I am Thine; save me!*"

Just let me illustrate this mistake by one of its highest but worst forms. I have seen more than one, who came to me with the pitiful, tearful, maudlin, half-crazed confession that they had committed "*the unpardonable sin.*" Oh, in my heart of hearts I pity those deluded and profane souls. I know it is often physical causes that lead to such thoughts; but the spiritual element is nothing but *pride and self-righteousnsss* There is no piety, no humility and no faith, in the boast of the "unpardonable sin." No past sin has ever kept a soul out of heaven, that would go to Jesus. It is Self, and the pride of self, that makes people value themselves and their feelings and experience so much that they say, "I am too much for Christ;" I have sinned away my day of grace, and therefore cannot, need not seek and sue for what He cannot and will not give. *He cannot? He* the Almighty God and Saviour? *He will not? He* the all-loving Jesus, the lover of our souls? And thus you charge upon

Christ the loss of your soul! His inability or unwillingness to save you, not upon yourself: *You* willing, anxious, in agony crying to be saved; and no help, no willingness, no power in Christ? Just think of it; what blasphemy! It is perfectly fearful how people can wrest the Scriptures to their own destruction. What has your past and your own miserable Christianity to do with your salvation? Count it all loss and come to Christ, who has said, "Him that cometh unto me I will in no wise cast out." Oh, *you are too great a sinner* even for Christ. Glorious pre-eminence among the poor herd of sinners whom Christ came to save. He and His sacrifice are not enough for you. You are *a special sinner?* No; you are just one like all others, that must come as a poor beggar and no more. God is no respecter of persons. What saved the Magdalen, what regenerated the publican is all you have to look to; there is nothing more powerful that is promised or possible. If the Gospel is good enough for any, it is good enough for you. Why, such people seem to glory in their especial sinfulness, and want God to do something "extra" for them; just as others plead their great intellect and philosophy and wisdom, to demand more evidences than the Scriptures give, and stronger motives than Christ's life and death and love. Whosoever it be, and whatsoever it be, just put away that *Self*, that *I*, which is constantly in your way. Kill it and put *Christ in its stead*; learn to look away from self; count your own peculiarities, preferences, excellencies, position, difficulties, etc., but loss, that you may find all in Christ, and from to-day trust Him, follow Him, serve Him, make Him your all.

> And be it so, that till this hour
> We never knew what faith has meant,
> Deceived by sin and Satan's power,
> Have never felt these hearts relent.
>
> What shall we do? Shall we lie down,
> Sink in despair and groan and die,
> And rest beneath the Almighty's frown,
> Nor glance one cheerful hope on high?
>
> Forbid it Saviour! To Thy grace
> As sinners, strangers, now we come,
> Among Thy saints we ask a place,
> For in Thy mercy there is room.

So trust Him! and He is yours, and *you are His*. Peace and strength will follow, the clouded mind be cleared, the foul heart cleansed. Humble yourselves; forget self; let Christ be all in all! and the battle is won, and you will know what power there is in the prayer "Lord I am Thine, save me;" and understand the declaration of the Gospel, "it is the power of God unto salvation to all that believe."

II. But this is only No. 1 of my text's lesson, free salvation. I must take up No. 2, *Work out*, (*not work, nor work for;* all that is Christ's;) WORK OUT *that free salvation.*

Man, the free agent, cannot be saved as a machine. He is honored to be God's co-worker, as in every purpose of life, so also in the work of salvation. All is freely given; but meetness must come, life must grow, acceptance be testified to, adoption be adopted *in our own life and heart.*

And brethren, if religion is worth anything, worth having at all, such must be its law.

Life! It is a passage from time to eternity. Like a ship bound to a foreign port, the ark of our life is bound for eternity, and that eternity has its two ports of entry and its two masters that own it. It steers for heaven or for hell, and it must show its papers of entry. It belongs to God or to the world, and must display the ensign "Lord I am Thine." Christians nail that flag to the mast, and follow the chart to the land of Holiness! or where will you drift?

Life is like a march of the army of God's creatures to the goal of heaven or hell; you must enlist in one body or the other. Hoist the colours of your Master Christ, and stand to your colours, or whose will you be?

Is not this the true point of the question? What

is religion, what is Christianity, what is the Church of Christ, what the services and the ministry worth, if they do not settle the issues of eternity, if they do not show in the life and conduct of Christians where they are from and whither they are going?

Is a mere half-way sort of religion worth living for, and worth the sacrifice of this world's idols? Is Christ's religion a mere ornament to be worn in the sight of an admiring or sneering world? A "dummy" to keep us respectable amidst the follies and excesses of the world? A morality without a divine regenerating principle, ministering to self and self-advancement and pride? A mere viaticum at the hour of death? Who can believe that?

Is it not the very soul-renewal from sin to holiness, the very rescue from sin to God? the absolute change and turn to renew, regenerate, re-fashion a man's inner and outer life, and make him fit for eternity and the Kingdom of God? to raise him to a new and higher sphere, and develop every latent power in him for what is godly, righteous, holy, true, honest and pure, and fit him for life here and for life eternal? *If not*, I say it in all reverence, it *is not worth having*, not worth living for, sacrificing for! Nothing at all! Worse than nothing, an impossibility. And those who think they can take it as a mere name to live and unite with it the love of the world, the lust of the eye, the lust of the flesh, and the pride of life; who can carry on both shoulders and now serve one and then the other, be loyal to both and the friends of both (ah! brethren, *is not that the precious so-called Christianity of thousands?*) they deceive themselves wofully, and have not gotten *the first entrance* into the narrow way that leadeth to life—*not the first!* " For what fellowship hath righteousness with unrighteousness?" and " what agreement hath the temple of God with idols?" *for ye, Christians, are the temple of the living God!*

Ah! Is there no work for the Christian? for him that has fled to Christ and saith "I am Thine?" No need for the cry "Lord save me?" and as a moral agent, to set to work and make his calling and election *sure, working out his own salvation?* Aye, *working out,* developing in his life, verifying, cultivating, nursing, working, harvesting, bringing out in his every thought and word and deed the great truth, " Lord, I am thine!" *Thine!* and therefore I, my heart, my will, my life, my time, my talent, my all I have and am—*Thine!*

Take that ship in which he is embarked! To reach the port must not every means be used? rudder, chart, compass, engine, speed—on, on, on! till the port is reached?

That march through a hostile world—does it not require circumspection, watchfulness, girding on the armour of righteousness to the right hand and to the left; armed cap-a-pie! and using that armour bravely, perseveringly, faithfully?

That life-work wherever it is cast, *must it not be done?* Is the way to heaven smoother in its working up to it, than the pitiful ways to earthly gains and accomplishments? —

Aye, I am not afraid now to add the sequel to my text, "work out your own salvation *with fear and trembling.*"

Powerful foes are abroad; within, without. Is it hard? All life, all labour is hard; nothing worth running for without sacrifice; nothing ours without the sweat of the brow.

Hard? No; for "it is God that worketh in us to will and to do!" It is still of grace.

As earthly means and instrumentalities and the wisdom of men guide us to success in the enterprizes of this life, so *God's Holy Spirit* is the power divine, to guide our souls unto salvation. And it is only a law of our nature that God ordains, when He saith to those upon whom He bestows His free salvation, "work it out." Work it out with fear and trembling, do it boldly, resolutely, whatever it may cost; hopefully and perseveringly, for "it is I who am working in you." Do you see the point of the Psalmist's cry, "Lord I am Thine, save me." *God saves us even in this.*

Wherefore "come out from among them," He saith. This is our part. Not come out from the circle of friends and brethren and neighbors, who shall teach you the lessons of love and human sympathy; "and be ye separate," not in monkish retirement and priestly dress, but separate from the ways and fashions out from the sins of the world. Show whose you are. It is not in phylacteries and the cut of the dress; not in badges, ritual and profession. It is in a purer life, a holier zeal, a more faithful obedience. It is in the inner depths of the heart, its desires and thoughts; in the heavenly conversation on earth and the loftier aims of the works. A higher righteousness, a nobler life, a deeper love, all for Christ and all in and by Him! Nothing impure and unholy to touch him; nothing selfish and low to drag him down; a heart to go out to all in love and sympathy and active benevolence as Christ's; a soul living in the presence of God and for His glory.

Here are your tests, and here your growth in Christ. And *that Christianity of yours* which is worthless as your justification, is trained into the most beautiful thing in all God's creation; *holiness* in thought and life, the express image of Christ Himself.

There are only two lives, the godly and the worldly; one only can we live, for no man can serve two masters. Hoist your flag and stand by it, and salvation shall be perfected in your training and discipline on earth. "With the heart man believeth unto righteousness, and with the mouth," with the evidences of our life, the visible witnesses of the outward life to the spiritual grace, even that faith within, "confession is made unto salvation."

Christianity begins in *a revolution:* the renouncing the bondage and breaking up the allegiance to the world, the flesh and the devil. But it trains into *a habit*, the perfect freedom of God's service.

"Lord I am Thine," the beginning.

"Lord save me," the continuing in the working out of what we have received, until the blessed end!

Its end: in the perfection and the glory of the world above! *and all is of God!—all of God!*

> My bark is wafted to the strand
>   By breath divine;
> And on the helm there rests a hand
>   Other than mine.
>
> One who has known in storms to sail,
>   I have on board;

Above the raving of the gale
   I hear my Lord.

      *   *   *

Safe to the land!—safe to the land!
   The end is this:
And then—with Him, go hand in hand,
   "Far into bliss!"

Whatsoever He saith unto you, do it.

Jno. ii. 5.

If I were asked to condense all practical teaching of the Scripture into one sentence, I would quote this text. For in one sense it is true: obedience, aye, obedience is the first and greatest lesson we draw from its revelation of the Saviour's relation to us and ours to Him, the pivot on which its every issue turns, the end towards which every result must lead.

Obedience—you ask? Is obedience to save us? does not all the Gospel preach *faith* as the means of acceptance and salvation?

Surely, my brethren, our obedience is never sufficient to work out our justification before God—"Christ is the end of the law for righteousness to every one that believeth." But it is not a dead faith, it is not a mere creed; nor is it mere devotion! It may come to us traditionally—and thank God generally and in His economy of the Church, it so comes to us, as we hear it at our mother's knees, and receive the promise of God's adoption in the baptismal covenant. But it must grow and become our own. And the knowledge of our own sinfulness and eternal soul-wants, must lead us *personally* to surrender to Him, and trust ourselves to His atoning power. It is the same faith, but the child is becoming a man. As we advance in life and experience, we learn what that means: "He came to save His people from their sins!" not only their guilt but their power! And by faith in Him, the living, working, struggling, sanctifying faith, we rise to the knowledge of His saving power, and *prove it in the obedience of the faith*, prove it by developing from it as the root that holy life without which we are none of His.

When the Apostle at the close of his life could say, "I have kept the faith," he meant, indeed, the faith involved in the first revelation of Christ to his soul as the alone Saviour; but as learned, practically, and exercised in a life in which he lived to Him that saved him, and followed His sinless, holy example, ever reaching forth for greater growth of His faith, more enlargement, grasp and power; more comprehension of it, by pressing towards the mark for the prize of the high calling of God in Christ Jesus.

Why, the true object of Christ's coming and dying for us was not to save us *in* our sins but *from* our sins; was and is, to lead us back to that obedience, and make it the habit and the joy and glory of our hearts and lives, without which no creature can live in God's world.

Obedience is the law of creation. It cannot be otherwise. If we live in a world of order, law, government, we must be in accord, in harmony with it; violation of its order, law and government is death, ruin, misery, exile!—Just think of inanimate nature. Let the sun, let the stars forsake their orbits—what follows, or would follow were that possible? Let the flower be deprived of the legitimate sources of its support and well-being, sunshine and dew, and it dies!—Let the animal be misled against its true instinct, it suffers and dies! And the moral creature, the free agent? Aye, he *can* disobey, but can he disobey without suffering, without "sin finding him out?" Man *can* choose, but he chooses wrong at his peril, and his only law of normal existence and possible happiness is *obedience*. He has fallen, hence his suffering and death; recovery made possible only by the Redeemer's merits and the sinner's faith in that Redeemer's work. Recovery remains an impossibility without the return to obedience.

Whatever people may say there are but two lines of conduct, but two roads of life. Man has the power to choose; but, with the road chosen, he must take the end to which each leads. He has no choice there; and the end of happiness, blessedness, eternal life is only in the road of right, truth and godliness.

The end corresponds with the road. Which is the right one? Which must we choose to be saved? Philosophers may twist and turn and try to avoid the issue, or deny our premises and conclusions as not scientifically demonstrable. But after all, there sleeps in every heart, there lives in every breast, the conviction and the knowledge that God presides over this world and over his own life and choice, and that only what *He* saith, what God and Christ say, is the right, the only road which leadeth unto life. I need say no more. If men are ostentatiously loud in proclaiming "the reign of physical law," and lay down obedience to that law as undeniable and imperative, they will not lower themselves by denying their higher nature and God's spiritual law, and refuse to obey that.

Whatever *He* saith, therefore, is our rule of life. And oh, He has said it so plainly in all His revelation of nature, in the invisible witness of our own hearts by the voice of conscience, and in the solemn and authentic revelation of His Holy Word.

The whole world is divided into but two classes. Those who obey that Rule or Law or Word, and those who do not.

Let us take the two classes:

There is one road, and over it is written "I came to do Thy will oh God, the will of My Father which is in Heaven." We might take the life of Enoch, of Noah, of Abraham, Moses, the Prophets, Apostles, Martyrs, of every Christian man and woman that lives, has lived and shall live in this world, but none are perfect. And we turn to the great example and forerunner of all righteousness, Jesus Christ, who came to earth *as man*, to show us how to obey the law of God and walk in the narrow path that leadeth unto life; not as God, but as man; not with divine power, but the power of pure, unsullied manhood; *the true Son of Man.* In His life we see our own. As He walked its rough and thorny road and toiled up its steep heights "holy, harmless, undefiled, and separate from sinners," but from that holy life on earth walked straight into heaven: so it is with all His followers; who after many a conflict and self-denial, and much crucifixion of the flesh, yet with many comforts and helps and promises, copy His bright example here and follow Him to the life of glory and bliss above.

There is the other road—and over it is written "who is the Lord that I should obey His voice?" I might speak of Adam and Eve in their fatal choice, of Cain, and a thousand others; but Pharaoh is a fair type, and his defiant cry the war-cry of those who walk in the broad road which leadeth to destruction.

You say, that is a hard saying, and that you do not accept his position. Does not every sinner do so? every one that rejects Christ? every one who neglects so great salvation?

Just think a moment. I know, few would use the words of Pharaoh, but—*act like him?* My dear brethren, I have known more than one who flatly refused to be Christians; who almost took offense at being approached on the subject, and at last closed the interview with an oath, "d— it! I don't mean to be a Christian!" I do not make an exaggerated statement, but I know it will grate fearfully on many a mind.

Well, if after all the lessons taught you, all the heart-burnings you have experienced, all the moments of hope and a better life you have had, all the urgent appeals, you just turn away: do you not say "*No, I won't!*"

There comes the call. Oh! in such love and tenderness and anxiety for your souls, and your happiness here and hereafter, and every comfort and blessing of earth and heaven—*No!*

There comes a temptation; you know it is wrong, sinful, deadly. Conscience speaks, all you ever learned comes back to your mind to warn you; examples of perishing sinners lift their pleading voices; God seems to be all but present and look into your very soul; Christ stands and pleads and points to His crown of thorns and cross of atonement: *No!*

Your old habits rule you. *No*, I cannot give them up, and you let go Christ! the idols of your life, pleasure, honour, riches. — *No*, I must worship them, and let go Christ!

Where is the difference? In the end, is there so much difference between Pilate saying "I see no fault in Him," yet delivering Him to His murderous enemies, or the Jews who crucified Him? between Ananias who lied to the Holy Ghost, and the young ruler who went away sorrowful, because he could not sacrifice his love of money for the salvation of his soul in the service of God and holiness?

Does not all turn on *practical faith, life, obedience?* aye, my brethren, the giving of the heart, which involves all life?

Two more remarks on the obedience we are speaking of:

1. It *must be instant*; delay is disobedience, and generally fatal disobedience!

All life teaches the sin and folly of procrastination! Let me give you an illustration from my own knowledge and recent experience.

A woman living in the country was taken desperately ill; the docter lived some miles off; she had had similar attacks before. Her only son was dispatched for the doctor. He thought, no doubt, it was one of her old attacks; he went off on his horse, rode at his ease, stopped at a neighbour's and paid a visit, and at last, leisurely reached the physician's home. I don't know if the doctor was in a greater hurry. Both came to the residence of the woman—*she was dead.*

Let me give you another illustration: A man is involved in debt, (how many have realized that condition!) It may be an individual, or a company, or a whole people; it does not change the issue or the principle. Let it be a man. Well! he may say, it is hard, hard; I don't see how I can manage it and save, even by close living and many self-denials and privations, enough to pay it; but it is an honest debt, a binding obligation. My debtors would suffer less by my dishonesty than I would do in my own conscience and sense of right before God and man! Of course it would be better, more pleasant, to do it right off; but if that is impossible, the instant obedience requires instant retrenchment, instant self-denial, instant endeavor to turn all into that channel. I have known a family that were unfortunate and failed. They set to work at once, and manfully, and I may say in a godly way; they lived on $50 a month (it was a large family) till they were clear. The children are living now, and God is prospering them in the world. That was instant obedience!

But there are others. What? to give up the life they are living and their position, and the things they are used to? it would be preposterous! And instead of trying how to pay their debts, year after year they use every ingenuity and every evasive plea and every plausible pretext to try, *how not* to pay their debt. Well, you may call it by a great many names, but in the sight of God and His law, it certainly is disobedience! God have mercy upon them!

And brethren, so it is in all things. These are mere illustrations. Any parleying with sin, any giving in, any postponing, is just that disobedience of which we are speaking now. "Oh! I am going to be a Christian?" *Are you?* I don't believe you; and *you* cannot believe it if you do not set to work about it at once, and be one, and as a poor sinner come to Christ and renounce your sins.

A dear and noble Christian friend sat by my fireside, a fugitive during the war. With all his trials he felt God's mercies gratefully; he turned to me and said, "yes I am resolved if God helps me through this, I am going to be a better man and serve Him more faithfully." I said, "why wait? why not do it right off?" He blushed, and said "Amen."

As long as you say *I am going to be*, there is no hope. You but make Christ the minister of sin, and fool your own self. Why, what keeps you? Are you honest in it? Can you plead the farm you have bought, the yoke of oxen you have not proved, the wife you have married? Ah! should not every claim of earth lead us nearer to God, and every tender tie of love lead us to bring with us to Christ the souls which He has given us?

I cannot dwell on the many miserable pleas made to excuse men's present disobedience. People can't believe the Bible, when they don't study it. Christ is such a hard Master? when He says my yoke is easy and my burden is light. Such a struggle! as if it were harder than the struggle of sin! — I am not prepared? when all that is needed is to go to Him. I am not good enough? when Christ came to save sinners, not the righteous. Shaw! What was the course St. Paul pursued? "Lord, *what wilt Thou have me to do?*" Can any reasonable, honourable soul excuse itself from that course? How was it with the Apostles? " Follow me," and they forsook all and followed Him. And whatever form it may assume, that is the only answer: *Instant obedience!*

Why, brethren, just take the question *of right!* Is it right? is it not sin to put it off, when we acknowledge the binding force of our obedience, and rob God of that much of our time and service? Yes, and take the question *of safety!* Putting off? *for what*—in comparison with what you refuse now? *Till when?* putting off—and with it you put off your chance, your time, your eternity! "Thou fool, this night thy soul shall be required of thee."

There was wonderful tact and insight into human nature in Dr. Chalmers' treatment of that young girl whose mother had complained to him that she could not persuade her child to be a Christian; that she had talked to her and talked, but it was of no use. He proposed that he should see her by herself. "They are bothering you a great deal with this question," he kindly said to her, "suppose I tell your mother you don't want to be talked to any more for a year—how will that do?" The girl stared at him with her large eyes in perfect wonder, and new thoughts seemed to come to her; she cast down her eyes and said tremblingly, she didn't think it would be safe to wait for a year, something might happen, she might die before that. "Well, that's so," replied the Doctor, "suppose we say six months." She didn't think that would be safe. "That's so, let us cut it down to three months." The girl looked down. "I don't think it would be safe to put it off three months: Doctor, I don't think it would be safe to put it off at all." And down they went on their knees, and it was settled.

There is no other way, my brethren; *now* is the accepted time, this is the day of salvation.

2. But, secondly, *obedience cheerful, willing*. There is no godly, no acceptable obedience without it. Suppose a man obeys from fear, from dread of punishment and hell-fire, does that change him? Change his mind, change his heart? Make holiness lovely and dear to him? Can any forced obedience live in heaven or be safe here? Will it not break down, will not the natural heart break through? The apostle says "the law was not made for a righteous man, but for the unrighteous." Why? Because the righteous is in harmony with the law, obeys it spontaneously and does not feel its restraints. As long as a man loves sin, he will find the service of God as a man finds the temperance pledge while the love of liquor is in him. It may restrain him for awhile, in the sight of others; he will be sure to give way to such temptations as

overrule his fears, and never be genial and happy in his constrained position. "Walk in the spirit and ye shall not fulfil the lusts of the flesh," is the Scripture-panacea. No, brethren, we cannot give it to ourselves, but God can give it to us—a love for Him and His holy ways—this conquers the heart, and with it, the man.

Oh! the burdened life, the struggles of the man that attempts to be *merely moral*, and neglects and refuses the spiritual power of Christ's Spirit, which alone gives freedom! and never rises to the liberty of the children of God, who, because children, count it their glory and privilege to live as such and be followers of God! Here is the point, and the only solution: We must have the heart for it, out of which are the issues of life. The heart, given to God; the heart, loving Christ: it must learn the lesson of purity and holiness and honesty and justice and truth. — Mere reformation is a legal burden and an all but certain failure! *Regeneration*, the birth of the soul into a higher and better and purer and heavenly life, carries with it the victory over sin, and the obedience of the faith.

It may be feeble, it may often be surprised, there may be states of lukewarmness, and sorrow over the momentary triumph of the adversary and our old nature. *But hold on! keep on! press on!* and the victory is certain. *God and Christ are pledged for it!*

Do it, do it at once, for ye know not what the morrow may bring forth.

Do it, as the craving of your better self, the living power of God in your soul.

Do it, in all things—" Whatsoever ye do, do all to the glory of God!" " Do all in the name of the Lord Jesus Christ!"

No man can serve two Masters.

MAT. vi. 24.

But why serve at all? and any body? Are we not free? — It is very certain we are free agents, *i. e.*, free to choose—but to choose what? To state it most generally, and without begging the question in behalf of my gospel, certainly between Right and Wrong: here is our responsibility and the price we have to pay for our freedom!

The first question then must be: what is right and what is wrong?

Wrong, logically stated, is "not right;" and this may be two-fold. *Negative*—failing to come up to what is right; *positive*—violating, transgressing, contradicting what is right.

The question resolves itself into "what is Right?" There must be a standard, and a perfect standard. Where is that absolute and perfect standard of Right?

1st. Is it *a man's own opinion and notions?* But they are various. The result of such a standard would disintegrate all moral life of humanity. On the plea of their own ideas of right and wrong, men could proclaim most contradictory standards, raised on their personal prejudices and views; and anarchy would rule.

2nd. *Is it the result of human legislation?* But is there, has there ever been, can there be a legislation of all mankind, a universal, all-commanding standard? Even if admitted, can it extend to anything but the act, the outward life? No one can see into another's heart. Man's law may, and must forbid "murder;" but is not hatred in the heart its source and main-spring? leading to the act, when opportunity is rife and temptation overpowering? Human law goes against "adultery," but is it not true that he that looketh on a woman to lust after her is guilty of adultery? Can human legislation meet that? — Thou shalt not "steal;" every human code of law provides against that; can it touch the covetous heart? the lying pretexts, the overreaching bargain?

So we go farther: 3rd. *The inborn sense of Right!* That indeed is a step forward, and leads to a higher view of man's nature, and a higher guide. All therefore admit the power and rule of *conscience*. But that does not, *by itself*, touch the standard of Right. Conscience is the authoritative and irrepressible arbiter within us; the voice of God, if you please, to approve or reprove what we do in agreement with or contradiction to what *we think is right*.

It is *not the judge of what is right or wrong in itself.* Countless are the cases in which men did what they held to be right, yet what was essentially wrong. On that ground the excesses and atrocities of all fanaticism could be justified. Conscience must be *educated* and *informed* by a standard, a perfect and absolute standard of Right; and *every holder of that conscience is responsible for every means to attain to that information.*

And thus there is admitted, beyond conscience and beside it, lying back of it, *an innate sense of Right and Wrong* as belonging to man and fixing the standard. If there is this "moral sense" brethren, then *it is given* by Him who made him; given, say, in the constitution which makes him a man, more so than reason given him above the instincts of brute creation.

But even this is not sufficient. (1.) There is against it the fact, the well-known fact, that this sense is not universally realized. And (2), all human experience—on the broad field of common humanity, as in the secret consciousness of the individual heart—proves that under the influence of habit, self-indulgence and sin, this standard loses its force, becomes biassed, dimmed, lowered, and is at last discarded, just as conscience can be "seared." All moral standards degenerate that are only under the control of man. And again, and more (3), even if not obliterated, coming only from man, it lacks that authority which alone could make it absolutely, universally and forever, the rule for each and all.

No, *we must look for the true standard of Right to* HIM *who created man.* In man's creation the supreme and necessary authority and standard is given.

That creation involves the existence, power and personality of God we do not argue now. Intellectual processes cannot prove it. The attacks on that ground by scientists are absurd. The Bible never claims that man could *see* God, and prove His existence and character by the evidence of the senses and natural proofs. But no philosophy has ever yet reasoned God out of man's heart and conscience, and never will, and with it His authority. The heart knows *there is a God;* and no sophism will succeed to abolish this evidence of consciousness, even after years of blating infidelity and defiant practical atheism. But if God made the world, the world is ruled by Him; not only physically, but morally. If we are His creatures, it follows that we must live under His law, and are responsible for obeying Him; and that *that only is right* which is in accordance with His will and His reign of physical and moral and spiritual Law!

I. *Here then is a Master;* and we must serve Him, or we fail in our very character as His creatures. Disobedience is ruin! Our naturalists are ready enough to hold up the madness of going against "the Reign of Law." Yes, but the reign of *His moral law*, given to moral beings, free agents, is infinitely greater and holier! This free choice lifts us to the highest rank of created beings, but it becomes fatal when abused. It needs no vindictiveness on the part of God to consign the disobedient to exile and misery. Death, whatever that be, destruction, must be the alternative of disobedience. God must rule, or the world falls to pieces. "I am the Lord Thy God, thou shalt have none other Gods but Me."

Here then is one service; God's truth, justice, holiness are, and must be, the conditions of life.

But brethren, falling short of it, violating His laws, (is not that the confession of mankind?) How do we stand in His service and towards this Creator and Lawgiver, who, by absolute necessity, must be our judge?—The love and mercy of God comes in here as a fact of revelation to complete the idea of God, our knowledge of Him; and the Master we serve, the God we must love and obey, is the Father of our Lord Jesus Christ. The son of God took upon Himself our sin and guilt, and made the reconciliation, that God "might be just, and yet the justifier of him that believeth in Jesus." *The atonement* ("at-one-ment"), to bring together what sin had severed—punish sin and save the sinner!

This God is our Master, and Him we must serve!

Serve? Yes, but this service is perfect freedom.

Let us understand this. Free agency is not freedom in the sense of absolute independence. As creatures we stand in a necessary relation to the Creator. As social beings we stand in as necessary a relation to our fellow creatures. And our freedom or liberty, large as it is in the aspirations and claims of the free agent, is limited by these two relations. Neither the dependence on the Creator, nor the state of co-existence with equals, allows of a freedom which would be anarchy and licentiousness. We may elect our course of action; but we must take its issues, and suffer if we make a wrong choice; suffer, because in our choice we either do right or do wrong. And "whatsoever a man soweth that must he reap," in strict accordance with the limitation by which his freedom is bounded in his position towards God and towards man.

Now, God's service is perfect freedom.

What constitutes freedom? Equality before the law; equal rights and privileges.

In God's service both are guarded:

1. "God is no respecter of persons."

2. "All ye are brethren," which involves the recognition of the mutual obligations between man and man, and in its highest sense prescribes the law of human life. Negatively—" Do that to no man which thou hatest." Positively—" Whatsoever ye would that men should do unto you, do ye even so to them."

Ah! brethren, more; that service is *not only free but blessed*. Blessed to us sinners, who accept, believe, serve their Master; for guilt is forgiven, and power given to return; no longer servants, but friends, children!

And such a Master! Can we deny Him?

II. But there is another Master that claims us, and carries thousands and tens of thousands in his bondage. Our Lord in the context saith; "ye cannot serve God and mammon;" that is to say, ye cannot serve God, and "not God," whatever that or he be. Mammon has been represented in many religious books as a Syrian deity opposed here to the true God. Such is not exactly the case, certainly not relevant. Wealth, riches, the world are personified by our Lord in the word "mammon." It is a mere representative of all that may draw the soul away from God. I know, that few things do so more than money if it is loved; but everything that is loved supremely, draws the soul away from God and becomes its destroyer. —

Now brethren, we have spoken of our relation to God and the service we owe Him. Surely it is a reasonable and just service, and one which must lead to happiness here and blessedness everlasting.

What is the service of mammon, earth, sin, self, the devil? Whilst the one is freedom, raising the soul to its highest goal and fulfilling its true destiny, the service of all else can only be slavery, bondage.

The service of sin! I do not know of anything more enslaving, more degrading! God knows I know enough of sin to feel for sinners, but it is just on that account I can speak, and must speak so positively.

It is downright slavery. The man cries "liberty," and does the very thing he has fought against and disapproves of, and knows will ruin him in time and in eternity.

A slavery which forces him to go against his own interest, against his conscience, against his fears, against his reason, against everything God has constituted as guardians to men's souls to keep them from ruin in time and in eternity.

Need I give examples? Just take the covetous, the ambitious, the pleasure-loving, the brutal sensualist, the drunkard. Ah, he knows he is doing wrong, ruining himself in health, reputation, everything, perhaps dragging down with him to misery and shame a lovely family. No! no! he will not, will not do it; he will reform! He will resist and never touch the cursed thing again! He takes an oath, he swears to God! — And the devil comes to him again and "he seeks it yet again!"

He that committeth sin is the servant of sin! Is it possible to deny, to disavow this? Aye, though they wake up from their trance of sin; though disappointment follow its every indulgence, and reaction be its penalty; though no prospect before to allure, no earthly, no heavenly hope or promise: the sin behind them goads them on; and they cannot, cannot leave its service, because they have lost all moral freedom, have lost the power to resist and live as they would.

III. No man can serve two masters.

Life too truly teaches us, there are these two masters. Can we make a compromise and serve both?

No, brethren. When Christ said "Ye cannot serve God and mammon," He did not deliver an exhortation, but made the statement of a fact, an absolute fact, about which cavil or doubt is impossible. Our Saviour does not warn us against the service of both, does not say "do not serve both, it is dangerous, it is wrong." He does not adjust the limits within which, the ratio in which, one can obey or serve the two; He simply avers *it is impossible* to serve both; one excludes the other; no man can do it!

It is a general principle, which is true—whether put in connexion with the subject of religion or anything else. The supreme place, and this is meant by the term "serve," (see the first and great commandment, "love God with all thy heart and soul and mind and strength,") that surrender of our affections and duties which involves all, cannot be divided. We cannot be the loyal and active subjects or citizens of two different countries or rulers. Two thoughts, affections, aims cannot co-exist for the time. "Of whatsoever a man is overcome, of the same is he brought into bondage." This is a fearful warning! And hence the great rule for a godly life "Walk in the spirit and ye shall not fulfil the lusts of the flesh." For no man can serve two masters. Therefore "if you are led by the spirit, then are ye the sons of God." — That service involves *the whole man*, his heart. God saith, "Give me thine heart," and the world says "give me thine heart;" and the poor man has but one heart to give.

Here is the common, I might almost say universal, error, (for who is wholly free from it?) that men think there is *a neutral ground* possible, a margin allowed; that there is a line of conduct which embraces both, in which we may partake of the service or the gifts of both; whilst the unalterable rule is "*either the one* or *the other.*" If the one, the other is impossible; one excludes the other. "If any man love the world, the love of the Father is not in him;" but if we are Christ's, "we have crucified the flesh with the affections and lusts thereof." —

Brethren, the text involves a great, an all-comprehensive principle. *Whatsoever* it be that divides the heart and draws it away from God, His love and service, it is that mammon which, by this pretended partnership in your heart, but seeks to ruin your soul. You cannot serve God and mammon (whatever that be in your case). And if this is true, I put it to yourselves, whether any man or woman in this house to-day can, in the sight of God, be in an equivocal position; can occupy a middle ground, a neutral position; whether there can be a state of indecision, halting, an "almost Christian" or an almost worldling; whether not all, if people cannot serve both at the same time, all here, must be either serving the one or the other?

I know people do not set out to turn from God entirely and give themselves into the worst of all slaveries. No; but if you serve the world and its lusts and aims, you actually have turned from God, for you cannot serve both.

Ah! in our unbelief of this great truth lies the secret of the ruin of so many, many souls, that even the hopeful heart of a Christian pastor is tempted to give them up as beyond the possibility of reach. As long as the world and its fashions are the idol, God is "unknown" and "unknowable!" The god of this world has blinded them, they cannot see and believe, and the secret of the failures which so many Christians seem to make in their relations, lies here. "There are thousands in our churches uncomfortable, ill at ease and dissatisfied with themselves, withdrawing from active church-work, they hardly know why; the reason is, they are trying to keep in with both sides." They are endeavouring to please God and to please man; to serve Christ and to serve the world at the same time; to claim His promises, but live in sin; to have treasures in Heaven and glut themselves with their treasures and pleasures on earth!

One thing is needful. One thing! as one Master! and one service! Attend to that first! and let God take care of the rest.

Let us be decided brethren, thorough-going, uncompromising followers of Christ. Let our motto be that of St. Paul: "one thing I do," to "press towards the mark." Our rule, that of Joshua: "whatever others do, however they may act, whatever service they may engage in, I and my house, we will serve the Lord!"

For Brethren:—You cannot be the friend of the world and the friend of God; you cannot serve God and mammon!

No man can serve two Masters.

The Lord is in His holy temple.

Ps. xi. 4.—Heb. ii. 20.

I. THE LORD IS IN HIS HOLY TEMPLE—*this glorious world, the great temple which God built Himself in the universe!*

By omnipotence the material was created, by wisdom its foundations were laid. Beauty built its walls, and goodness stored it with treasures, untold and inexhaustible. When it floated into being, the morning stars sung together, and all the sons of God shouted for joy; and throughout the ages of its continued existence, the visible things of His creation have made known the invisible things of the Creator, even His eternal power and Godhead.

The universe is God's great Cathedral; the azure dome with its golden stars above, the columns of His everlasting hills around, the wonders of bygone generations beneath. Armed with the telescope we see its aisles stretch along through the immensity of space till the computation of the distances makes the mind giddy, and yet beyond these are undiscovered stars and worlds of stars. By the aid of the microscope we discover a world beneath us, where the creative power of God is seen to write

His name on the very atom that is unappreciable to our mind but as an abstraction. And in the height and in the deep, in the greatest and the smallest of His works, wherever the eye glances we see the traces of a power and a wisdom which is divine. And when from the mechanism of the world and its architectural structure we rise to behold its dynamic and chemical forces, as we watch the returning seasons, the wind which bloweth where it listeth, the chemical affinities which in part we can trace and note; we see God at work! at work in the vast, the infinite house of His creation, weaving its coat of many colors and many forces and many blessings with an unwearied hand and ceaseless activity; supporting the whole in all-embracing laws, and guiding it by an ever-present will and energy. From all we see and do not see, from all we know and do not know, from all we have searched and do not and cannot search, the constant anthem rises of the whole creation to His praise and glory; the diapason of the deep, the thundering echoes of the height, day unto day uttering speech, night unto night showing knowledge: in more than pentecostal richness of tongues and languages and expressions, all His works praise Him and proclaim " The Lord is in His holy temple !"

Out of the field of His natural laws we rise to the

contemplation of the *moral* elements alive in His temple, and betokening His presence in His constant, overruling and sustaining *government* and *providence.*

Like a vast moving panaroma, the great Architect and Master has cast forth into existence the grand conception of His holy temple, this beauteous creation; and upon the world's canvass He has painted the history of its immortal inhabitant, placed there to fill the courts of His temple, and learn to worship with a living service their ever-present Lord and God. For six thousand years the great tableau of man's existence and history has been unrolled, and we cannot say how many ages yet may pass before the whole of God's work shall be complete in time. But who that traces back his steps, and casts his eye along the shifting scenes of this world-picture, as in uninterrupted flow they have succeeded each other; and watches their development and marks the causes and effects, as they combine at each period and lead us gradually to the scene which now stands before the eye of the beholder: but must see the golden thread of God's Providence interwoven with it all, and how all turns on the everlasting hinges of His government. *The history of the world* proclaims: "the Lord is in His holy temple."

The same is true of the life of the individual. Of all philosophies in the world the shallowest and most irrational, most degrading to the mind of man that honours itself in feeling after the high and holy God and forming an adequate conception of His attributes, the most puerile of all philosophies is that, which delegates to God what is called the general affairs and great outlines of the world's history, the first impetus in the play of its mental and moral elements; but denies His presence in the single events of life, denies the power of God and His presiding providence in that which forms the daily life and every hope of the individual!

Beloved, God's providence is like His creation. As the microscope discloses to us more of His creative power than the boldest flight along the stars that circle round us in unmeasurable orbits, so here, more than any where else, we see His ruling hand. For here we speak from experience and what our eyes have seen and our ears heard. Here in our every-day life, in our circumstances, our blessings, our trials, we see the presence of God. *We* are the inmates of that world which is God's temple; in Him we live and move and have our being. And of all the hopeless views and barren theories, his is saddest who lives "without God in the world!" — Here is the great lesson which we so constantly forget and lose sight of. "The Lord is in His holy temple;" but we forget His presence. Filling the whole universe, His mercies are over all His creatures; He is about our bed and our path; but we do not see Him, neither are thankful. He alone sends and controls the events of our life, but we live as if we were independent of Him, and rest in our own strength and make our calculations upon our own premises; and leave God out of the question—till He comes down upon us with a striking proof that His arm is not shortened. In that loss of a crop, when God drove the crushing chariot wheels of His hurricane across the field, or withheld the early and the latter rain from the farmer who left Him out of the account; in that failure which suddenly prostrates our business, which is based only on our own calculation; in that revolution which all at once changes the issues of public life, and cuts short the schemes of the politician, who cares for everything more than his God; in that sickness, which unexpectedly invades a family, that had been blessed with health so long that they looked upon it as their prescriptive right; in that vacant seat at the fireside, where, in the uninterrupted flow of prosperity, the family had forgotten that its blessings were a positive gift from God, and that He who was not thanked when He gave, would come to demand a blessing on His name as He took away: In these and other ways the Lord writes the proof of His presence and unceasing Providence in the life of every one of us. If we cannot read His hand-writing in the days of prosperity and rejoicing, we must thank Him when His chastenings and visitations lead us out of our godless state; and in every duty, in every trial, in the hour of joy or sorrow, to know to our great and endless comfort that "the Lord is in His holy temple," "the Lord God omnipotent reigneth!"

Without God in the world; without the sweet consciousness that we are living in His presence and under His watchful care; without the strength and encouragement for our work, which comes to us only when we feel that He is working with us; without that value of every blessing we enjoy, which only he can have that sees in it an instance of God's love; without His arm to support us in trials; without the comfort of going to Him when sorrow casts us down and all looks desolate and dark, of going to Him for help and consolation, and feel His gentle hand wipe our tears away; without the joy of praising Him for His goodness, and uniting with angels and archangels, with all His creatures of heaven and earth, in the exultant proclamation "the Lord is in His holy temple!" Oh, rather let me suffer the loss of all than not learn this lesson;

rather let the sun be blotted from the universe than the world for me to be without God!

II. "THE LORD IS IN HIS HOLY TEMPLE," *His Church!*

The world, the universe speak to us of *the Creator*, the Church *of Christ*. It is the world of the Redeemed, of those who having wandered from their home in the Father's love and strayed in the ways of sin and fallen under the sentence of death, are recalled by grace to return to God as penitents, trusting themselves to the mediating power of Christ.

As we watch the course of history and the development of our race, we find this Church the company of the faithful everywhere, and its destiny, preservation, guidance and growth the great idea and object underlying all the dealings of God with man. "Behold, I am with you always," is but another form of our text "The Lord is in His holy temple."

Oh, brethren! it is a fearful thing to be without God in the world, but it is perfectly awful to *be without God in the Church*. Our whole life here is one of probation. We are probationers for eternity; this whole world is but made for the saints. God has established His Church on earth, to train us as candidates for immortality, to prepare us for heaven.

Eternity is before all. Heaven only for those who are members of the Church of Redemption, with whom God resides as Immanuel. And oh! *to be in this Church, in this Christianized world, and yet without God! To be in this world without Christ!*

To call together His elect and train them amidst the temptations of the world and their conflict with evil for their heavenly inheritance, the Church has been established visibly among men, with appointed means and ordinances which were sanctioned as the blessed means to uphold and build up the spiritual edifice of the Church, and *in them we see again how "the Lord is in His holy temple."*

As He has hallowed the Sabbath day, so He has hallowed the courts of His sanctuary. Here, even in these walls, here is God; He is now in His holy temple. The promise that "where two or three are gathered together, there am I in the midst of them," the great pledge "in this house will I give peace," are ours *here* and *now*. Oh! it is not without meaning or spiritual confirmation that the minister dismisses you with "the peace of God which passes all understanding;" for here we are led to Him who is our peace. How the annals of mankind could bear witness to this fact, and how without these means and their use, religion becomes extinct!

Does not your own experience, does not your own practice bear the same testimony? Is not this house, for many, a house of mercy? And this day and these ordinances the very joy and strength of many souls? It is very true, beloved, these are but as the scaffolding of the true spiritual edifice where God dwells. But to us they are of infinite importance. God would not have ordained them if they were not needed for us; and wherever they are neglected (let history and experience testify) the Spirit, too, departs, and God's presence is withdrawn. We, indeed, must worship Him in spirit and in truth; but only those worship God spiritually and truly, who with an humble and believing mind confess Him in His own terms, seek the assistance of every means of grace and rejoice in these "vestiges" of His saving, sanctifying presence. No, my brethren! where the heart is set on God, where Christ is the hope of the soul, His way in the sanctuary is the very joy of the believer; and it *is just as awful to be without* CHRIST *in the* WORLD *as to be without* GOD *in the* CHURCH!

III. "THE LORD IS IN HIS HOLY TEMPLE!" I am coming to my climax.

From God and His creation we have risen to His spiritual temple—the church of Christ; but *the Holy of Holies*, where God resides most intimately, *the most sacred temple of the living God,* is *the human soul, the soul of the believing, faithful Christian.* "Know ye not, saith the apostle, that ye are the temple of the living God?"

I know of no truth so sublime, as that we are the temples of the Holy Ghost; that God the High and Holy one who inhabiteth eternity, also dwells with the humble and contrite soul; that as Christ tabernacled in the flesh, He now tabernacles by His spirit in every believer's breast. There is a divinity in man on earth, and every converted soul has it; but it is not the native grandeur of our souls, and the strength of our own goodness and power. It is *Christ in us!* It is *the gift of God's Holy Spirit* which every truly converted soul possesses. *Of every Christian, but of the Christian only* it can be said "the Lord is in His holy temple!"

Here is just the point. This world is God's handiwork; the temple He built Himself in infinite space, abounding with the proofs and tokens of His power, wisdom, goodness; and even in this world, which lieth in evil, He resides as in His temple; His omnipotence and providence uphold and govern it, and make the wrath of man to praise Him!

The Church on earth is the company of all believers, and as a visible society it is led on and presided over by the Lord our God. He who redeemed it, dwells in it to guide and bless and sanctify it, and conduct it safely towards the day of final triumph.

Still all this is more general in its bearing, in the aggregate as it were. But religion and Christianity are personal matters, matters of each individual, matters between the soul and God! And therefore our own hearts must be the temples of God; the spirit of God must dwell in us, or we are none of His! This is more than the Church of the redeemed, it is *the Church of the sons of God.*

Let me then ask you, is He, *is* He in your hearts? Are you not only of the number of those who profess the religion of Jesus and confess His name as alone saving; but, have you received Him in your hearts? Is he the God enthroned there? Can you hope that you are a temple of His holy spirit? Ah! I know, every heart is a temple. But what God dwells there? Is it the Lord or the world? Is it some evil passion or the holy Jesus? Is it the spirit of earth and earthly things, or, is it the spirit of Holiness and godly love? This is a vital question for us all, for every man and woman born into this world—for you and for me. All of our religion is of no use, unless Christ is ours and we are His. All the glories of God's temple and our acknowledging Him in the world, all the blessings of

His church and our joining it, are nothing, and worse than nothing, unless our hearts are His and there He resides as the Lord our God, our Saviour, our Sanctifier.

I am sure I am saying what every one can understand. We do not demand mystical and supernatural proofs and signs. Let all ask themselves, what is the bias of my mind; what is the principle which rules my thoughts and words and actions; what is the object of my life? Is it holiness, or is it the acquisition of some earthly good, the passing gains of this life? Which do I seek first and most anxiously; what is the will and the law and the spirit that rules me? — Self and the world, or God and Christ? This is the test of the Christian, beloved, that our heart be set upon God and godliness; that whatsoever we do, we do all to His glory; that the goal we run for be holiness, likeness to Christ; that we stand not in our own will, but the will of God, and study to live up to our prayer "Thy will be done." These are the proofs that we are God's, living members of His Church; that not only our bodies and souls are fashioned by Him, and under the power of His sovereign Providence; that not only we are sprinkled with the blood of Christ for justification so as to escape hell: but that *we are new creatures in Him*, spiritually-minded, growing more and more into His own image and living the life of God on earth. *Thus we are the temples of the Lord*, and thus only our foreheads bear the inscription, "The Lord is in His holy temple." — But oh, the alternative! *Without* GOD *in the* HEART, *without the* HOLY GHOST *in the* WORLD, it were better for us had we never been born!

IV. THE LORD IS IN HIS HOLY TEMPLE! *Heaven, God's throne!* That better world above, where sin is not known and where we shall see even as we are seen!

Ah, my brethren! if we are the temples of God here, if Christ dwells in our hearts by faith, if we have the unction of His Holy Spirit, His greater temple must be ours too. The Church of Christ, the family of God, is but one in heaven and earth. It can add but little; for eternal life is ours now. We have commenced it here. Having the Holy Spirit of God residing in us, we are already sealed as the inheritors of His house above. The veil of flesh and blood may shroud it from our view and actual enjoyment. There is a great difference between the anticipation of faith and hope, and the full blaze of sight and the riches of fruition. But it is ours, even now; ours by faith, as really as if we beheld it by sight. And we are already in possession of its best gifts, the love and communion of God. After all, the presence of God is heaven must still be of a spiritual nature, just as it is now—" flesh and blood cannot inherit the kingdom of God." The difference is, that here our spiritual sight and faculties are obscured by the associations of earth and the remnants of sin. But all these hindrances shall be removed, that veil which still hangs between us and our entrance into glory shall be rent—*and then?* Ah! in this thought is opened to us the scripture, that death shall be destroyed and the grave be swallowed up in victory—*and then?* It is more the Lord coming to His own, to those in whose heart He already reigns, and whose love is His already; coming to them with the last and everlasting blessing of His love and presence, than our coming to Him and entering into new life! *and then? then!*

You have seen the child awaiting his father? they had been separated long; sea and land were stretched between them. But after his long absence he is announced as returning to abide with them and bless them with his constant presence. Weeks are counted after weeks, and then days after days, and hour after hour. The moment draws nigh. See how that child becomes all expectation; the playthings which had engaged him before, are thrown aside; the face glows in new radiance as he looks forward to the joyous moment—his whole soul seems to be wrapt in anticipation! He listens to every step! At last—oh! notice how he starts! At last, that step is heard. The child knows it, knows his own father's tread, knows it instinctively, knows it by love! Ah, that father was his already. His love was his, and no doubt ever flashed upon his mind as if his affection could have been lessened, and their reunion cannot make those ties more endearing, their bond firmer! And yet—have you never seen such a scene? How he trembles in momentary expectation; how all is forgotten, but his coming father; how he looks out as if he had never seen him before; how he stands breathless and with palpitating heart! Nearer comes the step, and nearer: he is already mounting—at length—the door opens, *and the child springs into his father's arms!*

Such is the ascent of the believing soul into the temple of temples—his Father's arms!

God who, at sundry times and in diverse manners, spake in times past unto the fathers by the prophets, has, in these last days, spoken to us by His Son.

HEBREWS i. 12.

It certainly is a blessed, and, I think, upon the premises of the world as it is, an all but necessary fact, that God should speak in a particular manner by positive revelation to a particular people, whom, in a fallen and corrupt world, " until the fulness of time should come," He constituted the keepers of His oracles. But that does not exclude a farther and undeniable truth, that God has spoken, not only to Israel and the fathers of the covenant, but in diverse manners, though not in the same way as to His chosen people, to all mankind, in every age and condition.

That the Creator should care for the creature is shown, not only in the physical world, but is involved in our very conception of Him and the relation existing between the two, the Creator and His creation. We would say it is the natural and inalienable claim of the creature, the moral creature certainly, to a moral, righteous Creator. Do not fear that in saying this we are violating our reverence and creature-dependence towards the omnipotent God, "the potsherd striving with Him that fashioned it," the child saying to the parent, "what hast thou brought forth?" No, we are respecting God's own work and creation that came from His hand "good and upright," "made in the image of God." In that image (all the more, because lost in the fall) we more than trace our intuitions of right and wrong *to His own character.* The Scriptures certainly uphold this view throughout. "He is not a God of the Jews only, but also of the Gentiles." "He was in the world but the world knew Him not." Every false religion but denied the truth; forgot, degraded it from what it was in the first purity of their existence, and is a perversion and apostasy "when they knew God they glorified Him not as God, who changed the truth of God into a lie and worshipped the creature more than the Creator."

My brethren, all history proves this, and is the record of man's consciousness of his connexion with God. The one fact of man's sense of accountability proves it; and shows how everywhere and in all times man, this creature of earth, has been struggling up, groping, "feeling" his way (is not that St. Paul's statement in the Areopagus at Athens?) towards, and aspiring to communion with God;

and realized, whether in fear or hope, the presence of that God, without whom his life rests on nothing, defeats his search into cause and effect, and has no aim but the enjoyment or endurance of the fleeting moment, *the life of the brute.*

The idea of God is found everywhere, among all men, a higher and controlling Being. Whether this thought, or the results of this thought, are given in his constitution or by special revelation, need not trouble us; it comes to the same thing. For that constitution and all its intuitions—the inate ideas so much deprecated by philosphers—come from Him who created man and (ah! here again comes in the wonderful and unique testimony of Scripture) were given him by God "breathing into his nostrils," as He did to no other creature, and then "man became a living soul," differing, radically differing, from all others, as a living, rational, immortal, and accountable being. Or it may be traced back to the first and never-forgotten reminiscences of his paradisial days in Eden, when man walked with God (hence all the traditions of "a golden age") a consciousness as ineradicable as the sense of sin in fallen man. It makes no material difference in the main question. But we cannot overlook the remarkable fact that the knowledge, the worship and the fear of God—*some God*—are universal. No exception to this has ever been *established.**

But more than that. Secondly: Everywhere we find the sense of sin and the need of atonement and sacrifices, with a view to that. More still; a representation either of the God to appease, or the God-like powers to fight off the wrath of the offended deity, like the *Dii Averrunci* of antiquity, as most Fetishes are and modern superstitions. All form a testimony on the part of man's consciousness, which establishes the Apostle's words, both that "He hath made of one blood all nations of men," and also "that they should seek the Lord," "feel after" the incarnate God, whom they vainly and rudely and superstitiously sought in the elements of nature, in the stars of the seasons, or even the wood and stone of their Fetishes.

Let me pass before you the leading types of all man's religion.

I am not one of those who believe that man

---

* So many, such disproportionate majorities of so-called primitive races, as opposed to the very few exceptional cases reported by passing, shallow, uninformed, and prejudiced travelers, represented by them to be without the knowledge of God and religious rites, (after all but the results of original religious feeling,) have been proved to be worshippers of a God or higher beings, that the conclusion is overwhelming, the induction perfect, as regards the few whose condition may yet be allowed to be unproved.

was evolved from either the ape or the savage. The first position seems already passing away, and the materialistic evolution-theory must meet with the fate of "the vestiges of creation" which years ago made weak-kneed Christians tremble. I think their day must come! Science goes against them, must go against them. The missing link is missing every where, the growth of one species into another denied by nature's proofs, the spiritual apart from the natural undeniable.

As to man's starting as a savage? It is utterly incomprehensible to me how sensible men can still uphold anything approaching that view, and follow the guidance of men like Tylor, Buckle and others. We might as well listen to the sentimental twaddle of J. J. Rousseau, and worship the savage as the perfection of man. Of course we do not claim for that first race what we now call the refinements, and what are the artificialities of the present day. Such have been different in all ages, and even the superlative luxury of Rome in the dissolute and reckless days of her wretched empire, was very different from, and as in many respects far below, so in others far ahead of the so-called comforts, and the things which from artificial luxuries have almost passed into the "matter of course" and "necessary" things of our days. But Savages four thousand five hundred years ago? when all science confirms history, and has proved that no traces of human life are found farther back than that! Savages, in that moment of time, to have risen into the civilization, which built the tower of Babel and the pyramids of Egypt, which constructed the canals of the Nile and the Euphrates, and stood forth as thoroughly, thoroughly organized states, priestly, military, civilly, commercially, mechanically, agriculturally? There was not time for such development, evolution, if you please, of the savage.

Unless the descendents of Adam, made in the image of God, though fallen into sin and depravity, retained some of the original powers with which man was endowed to fit him for the dominion of this earth; unless, as compared with the fallen, and since then naturally and ever degenerating races of the earth, there had been, in Scripture-language, "giants in those days," why all history would be unintelligible, all advance an impossibility! Unless aided from above or outside, the development of man is downward! reason shows it, the facts of the savage world show it. Once let sin and godlessness seize upon the world, and the downward course is fearful, till it reaches the bottom in the worst specimens of savage life; the hopeless, unprogressive, undeveloping, *unevolutional, stationary* status of barbarism, whose rise into a higher life of thought and aims becomes a kind of resurrection. But all history, (historical, actual facts, not hypothesis, not preconceived so-called "theory,") proves that there is no new life, no new thought, no resurrection to a higher state, unless by influences from abroad; by races or men of higher endowment; and if we go back to the root, *by a revelation from on high!*

Let me lead before you the main types of religious life. Even in that state of degeneracy, the idea of some higher being or beings is not lost. It always prevails. If not the one Holy God, the one ultimate, philosophical, truly religious and only cause of all: every where we find at least *the second causes*, that became multiplied according to men's wants, their hopes and fears, (the true source of man's "many lords" and "many gods," developed from the original monotheism of mankind,) and which resulted in what is now called *animism*; that is, the peopling of the world with spirits and ghosts to affect and control the life; spirits of the air, spirits and ghosts of the departed, spirits of life and of death; the sprites of sky, water, fire and earth, the elves of the woods and meadows, the gnomes of the mountain caves and the mines of the earth, that in all were working for the weal or woe of those who dealt kindly towards them, or had to conciliate their enmity. Ah! the spectre and ghost-religion of the savage! it lays hold of "the savage" in all mankind! and peoples our childhood with superstition, and foists itself upon men in the fetishes of the savage, the hallucinations of astrology, the witchcraft of mediæval times, the table-turnings and the monstrous, so-called spiritualisms of the day! It is a return in the midst of the broad light of the nineteenth century to the idols of the barbarous mind; and only shows how man is wedded to the inscrutable, the unintelligible and the mysterious; and how, if he will not believe the truth, he believes a lie.

But let us pass to the intelligent races of man, that had not sunk so low, nor lost the vestiges of a true God! Whether we take the different fables and mythologies of the nations of the earth (which all make up the religious history of man's moral and intelligent nature) and their exposition in the ceremonies and rites of their worship (embodying their fears and hopes, their higher and lower standard); or, whether we examine the speculations of the sages and masters of mankind, from the earliest days down to our own times, in their presumed, and perhaps often only dialectic and vain boast of the progress of thought: the key to the understanding of all, the question proposed and the answer sought in all, the reaching out of the mind and heart of every man—is just the mutual relation between the Creator and the creature, the absolute necessity of harmony between the two, to make existence normal and intelligible. For sinners—a reconciliation with God; for moral, spiritual beings—an identification with Him in will and nature. Humanity is an unsolved riddle without this harmony assured. This is the "beginning, middle and end" of all the intellectual as all the moral life of Humanity!

This being so (and, I apprehend, no intelligent hearer, no one who has read history and studied the development of man's mind and heart, no one who has risen to higher aspirations than the passing things of this world can deny it,) it strikes me that *the admission of Christianity as its all-sufficient, and alone satisfactory solution, is a foregone conclusion!*

I come back to the text from which I started. I am free to confess, that in my own opinion the idea of God itself is *given* to man, who could not have reasoned above his premises; given, as admitted already, either in his mental and moral constitution, the work of God's hand; or, as a primitive revelation, (and I forbear now to show how much there is in favour of that)* and perhaps the memory, linger-

---

* The question here touched upon is fundamental. It embraces the question of the origin of all human civilization, of which the knowledge of God is the beginning. If it owes its origin to the

ing in the heart of paradisial days, when before the trial and the fall God and man were at one. In this same way I can ascribe the solution of this life-question—the reconciliation of man with God, and man's return to Him as pardoned and sanctified—I can ascribe it to nothing but God's own mercy and power; and therefore find in all these aspirations, feelings and struggles of man, *a response to the voice of God that resounds and has resounded in the hearts and minds of all!*

One thing is all but incomprehensible to me— that intelligent and upright men, men who have studied the history of our race, its outward growth and inward development, and who are capable of

---

creature, if it is the result of the premises contained in him and his constitution, why should it not reach perfection, and in the process of its evolution, go on forever growing? Instead of which we find, it ever fails and falls. But when connected in its origin with the teaching and the knowledge of God, conveyed to him by an external revelation, which in the power of his free agency he was capable of accepting and obeying, or to reject and disobey; then, whilst the high powers with which man is endowed allow him, under favourable circumstances, when once taught, to retain it to some extent and carry it on to a certain height; yet, when cut off (as is the case in the God-alienated creature,) when cut off from the knowledge and love and dependence of God, it must become mortal like himself and liable to deterioration and decay. And with the loss of Christianity—the revealed religion—barbarism must be its ultimate bound.

seizing upon the points at issue; who have dived into the mysteries of man's inner life, and (unconsciously perhaps) implied the need of belief in their very skepticism as to any proposed philosophical system: how they can, for one moment, hesitate to accept the revelations of Christianity over all the chimerical and fanciful attempts of speculation or conceits of other and present ages, and even what we so fondly style "the progress of modern thought" and "the highest efforts of the human mind!"

Given: a perfect and holy God, the almighty infinite Creator; and the finite imperfect creature, made fatally imperfect by sin! (I have the right to take these two premises; without them there is no common ground, no reasoning on the question.) How can harmony be brought about? That harmony which is the effect, the "feeling" of all? How can reconciliation be effected, acceptance procured, man raised to the image of God?

I stand on my right and the premises of man, (God forgive me if I am wrong) but I think I am within the limits of reason, nature and Scripture.

It must be either a descent from God to man, or an ascent from man to God; and we will soon see, to bring about the harmony, it must be both, *God in man* and *man in God.* But before we reach this, one thing is necessary, or the attempt is useless.

For man, free man, God's image, cannot be saved as a machine! The rights, if I may say so, of *both parties*, must be saved. *God's holiness and sovereignty*, and *man's personality and moral agency*—or both would be degraded.

Now what do we find? We pass the animism of ancient and modern times and delusions? What do we find in the best products of human speculation? "The little birds sing east and the little birds sing west!" it is the same all through—the east and the west.

The dreamy east,—take its highest representation in Hindoo Brahmanism: it sinks the man and his personality in the absolute impersonal deity (after all the fleeting phenomena of earth and caste, ascetism and transmigration, that is the great consummation and boast, "I am Brahma!"), in the absorption of the creature in the absolute essence; which *in Buddhism*, the pet of modern sentimentalism and Broad-churchism (at best, and with all its enlarged liberty of man as man, the *most complete pessimism* as it seems to me), becomes "the *still-life in an unconscious Nirvana!*"

The polytheistic religions of the west began at the opposite end. Instead of divinity coming down to men in partial and irrational, and to my mind profane emanations (assuming the divinity capable of losing more and more of the divine perfections) in avatars or manifestations, incorporations, external overcomings of man, partial and temporary, they begin with man's aspirations, and in seeking God, deify Humanity. They magnify man in his strivings and conceptions, and raise an earthly and earth-born Olympus; they clothe the gods with whom they live (still a communion with God!) in the sins and imperfections of man:— God in man's image, not man in God's!

And the highest philosophies which men have attempted from the days of Pythagoras and Anaximander and even the disciples of Socrates, fail still more *in sinking both* God and man. All pantheistic, giving us at best a *world-soul*, robbing us of the personal God; and which in their most daring development of "anthropotheism," identify man and God *in essence*, making God the product of man's conception and process of reasoning, the evolution of human thought, coming into being in that process! And though it is true that many of his startled successors have shrunk from following the leadership of Hegel, yet as I understand it, he has laid open the main-spring and given the key-note of all transcendentalism. Wearied, disappointed and hopeless, the soul returns from its vain search for truth and peace in the barren fields of such speculations, that all reduce themselves to the philosophy of "no God;" and finds life, hope, light only *as it bows at the name of the incarnate God.*

[The evolution-theory of these days, the natural progress in the survival of the strongest and best, an ever-growing perfectibility *out of itself!* — Apart from its impossibility, according to the facts of life and nature—why, at last, man by evolution will reach divinity! Is it so? How long will it take? And what of those ages before us; and when shall it at last be realized? And what becomes of *present salvation*, to us and our generation? Millions of years hence the imperfect mortal evolving into divinity! I have no fear of this impossible evolution-theory, nor the absurdity of mere matter rising into spirituality and divine life, except for those who are its temporary victims, who seek their promised divinity in the low-grounds of earthliness and materialism, (the worst of all degrading creeds, akin in philosophy and religion to a political creed, which would take for its main and cardinal principle the sentiment, that "honour does not get a breakfast.") Humanity will not stand it, it seeks a present salvation, its goal is immortality and God!].

Even apart from religion, is there any rest in such speculations? *Have you found your God?* Has your intellect met with its resting-place? your heart been touched, your moral nature been raised? More: Is it *religion?* God and man in mutual relation of care and dependence? And yet, does not religion alone meet the cravings of the heart, and is the Christian religion less philosophical? Is it not more true than all?

A descent of the Godhead, an ascent of man!

God coming down, but not to abolish personality, nor work salvation by merely appearing on earth without assuming and identifying Himself with man's nature.

Man's ascent, but on the wings of faith, and the new and divine nature given.

A true union, God in man and man in God; as the Scripture hath it, "*God manifest in the flesh,*" "*man partaker of the divine nature.*"

I pass Christ Himself. No one can answer the argument from His life, character, doctrine, work.

But take Christianity to solve these questions. As God created man, so God alone can re-create him after the fall, and restore him to His communion by His own almighty act!

Ah! that act of omniptence! That act of love, rushing forth from His heart of love to create and re-create a world, capable of loving and being loved. A love to save, to redeem, to win back; a love to suffer and die for the redemption, the recovery of the race so nobly born as to be able to choose, capable to err, yet to return, believe and love. A God to unite with the cherished work of His hands, to give Himself for its redemption, and raise the creature in the arms of the Creator's love; give it again His own image, make it a partaker of the Divine nature; and therein find His highest act of love, and therein reveal the almighty act of wisdom and power *which made the impossible possible!* Can anything else bring satisfaction, hope, peace? —

My brethren, the two items or facts in this whole question are: God's holiness and man's sin. The discord thus existing, this gulf between the two, is not only an undeniable fact of consciousness, but is *an eternal* fact, unless there comes in another fact, *the fact of reconciliation;* and that upon grounds of guarding the rights and properties of both, and meeting the issues by absolute right and justice.

Now—there is man's sin—*merit* only can expiate, can cancel it in God's eternal court of perfect justice; merit alone can become its equivalent, its substitute. Only God can possess merit, and do more than duty requires, duty demands—not of God, but of His creatures. Is there any way but that of the Gospel? which proclaims, not only the actuality of the atonement, but that this is *God's eternal decree and act of love!* "God so loved the world that He gave

His only begotten Son;" and out of that recess of infinite, unbounded, unfathomable love came forth *the mission of Christ:* The Son, to die in expiation of the creature's guilt that believes in Him, and to rise again for our justification; to reveal and manifest this invisible God and His unknown love, and bind together God and man in new and eternal union!

The atonement must be a divine act, the substitute a divine Saviour; or there is no possibility of salvation. *Yet, as substitute,* He *must be man,* "very man," or the case is not touched. Otherwise what hope of salvation and religion, in view of God's holiness and justice? in view of man's wants? Ah! is not this justice and holiness and mercy, which all humanity claims, just bound up in God's *first love?* and realized in *His incarnation?* His incarnation in man? Accepting it in faith, *i. e.,* utter renunciation of our own righteousness, *alone can make it ours.*

But let us not forget this: God necessarily requires *a perfect manhood,* not only that man should bear the penalty, but that man should be raised into communion and fellowship with God! God requires it; Christ requires it; we require it, reason demands it and Christ gave it.

The divine substitute not only brought the expiation, made the needful sacrifice as man, but *as the Son of Man* in His perfect obedience to God and perfect representation of God's image in man, *restored the character of the creature*, and raised it to the possibility of enjoying God's presence in heaven, whose law is God's will and God's will the joy of His creatures! *Here is the power of Christ*, to make us the children of God, proclaiming His Fatherhood, to educate and elevate us to the life of God, "purged from our old sins," "partakers of the nature of God," to a common and eternal brotherhood "all ye are brethren," to have "fellowship with the Father and Son and fellowship one with another."

Thus we have *the perfect sacrifice, the perfect humanity!* And *in the incarnation*, every mystery and doubt and impossibility solved and settled.

I have finished, I have no appeal to make, but only call the witnesses.*

Reason!—it bows in adoration before the truth as revealed in Jesus. I will not quote the well-known sayings of Rousseau and Napoleon, so constantly hawked about but not very relevant. The coryphees of speculative philosophy—Spinoza, Kant, Schelling, Hegel—all, however inconsistent in their

---

* Cf. Geike, Life of Christ, Preface and Introduction.

impersonal and pantheistic views, throw their crowns at the feet of Christ, and find in Him alone (I quote their own words) "the divine wisdom," the "perfect ideal;" aye, "the union of the divine and human." And the most critical of German Rationalists, (the representative of their better school, De-Wette,) in his last utterances professed: "This only I know, that there is salvation in no other name than in the name of Jesus Christ the Crucified; and that nothing loftier offers itself to humanity, than the God-manhood realized in Him and the Kingdom of God which He founded."

History!—all along—the testimony to Christ! Pointing (to use the words of Jean Paul) to Him, who, being the Holiest among the Mighty, the Mightest among the Holy, lifted with His pierced hands empires off their hinges, and turned the stream of centuries out of its channel, and still governs the ages.

Experience!—it passes unsatisfied the "cisterns, broken cisterns," of man's philosophy; and to quench his undying thirst, leads to the "well of living waters," which in the gospel springs up into life eternal, "He that drinketh of it shall thirst no more."

Experience which teaches that all else is perishable, every power and every force of earth passing away; the empires of its Alexanders, Cæsars and Napoleons tumbling to pieces, but the religion of the Carpenter of Nazareth stands and grows, "and millions this day are ready to die for Him!"

Conscience! impossible to be touched by intellectual philosophy, and responding only to religion! In the ever-living words of St. Paul "the gospel by the manifestation of the truth," (the truth as revealed by, and in Christ,) "commending itself to every man's conscience in the sight of God"—can anything else appeal to man's conscience?

Morality! Ah, "to be a perfect Christian is to be a sinless man!" Sinless through the obedience of perfect love. What a standard! What a calling! God's law not only the rule, but the choice, the joy and glory of the heart!

"Love, says one, has no diviner emblem than the good shepherd. Beneficence, no ideal so perfect as that "it is more blessed to give than to rereive." Fidelity to duty no loftier standard than a life laid down at its command. Self-sacrifice no dream so perfect as the record of Christ's death upon the cross."

And we may add, *communion with God?* No meetness but, "blessed are the pure in heart, for they shall see God."

Eternal life and immortality? Assurance only in

the source of life, in Him "who hath the words of everlasting life, and brought life and immortality to light through His gospel."

To believe in Jesus, the divine Saviour, IS LIFE EVERLASTING.

To know Him is to have PEACE WITH GOD!

AMEN and AMEN!

What have I to do any more with idols?

Hos. xiv. 8.

In Gibeon the Lord appeared to Solomon in a dream by night; and God said, "Ask what I shall give thee." And Solomon asked not for himself long life or riches or power, but "an understanding heart, to discern between good and bad." And it pleased the Lord, so adds the sacred record, that he had asked this thing.

Let that choice be offered to you, brethren, and say, as in the sight of God, *what you would ask for.*

It is sad to think how much we live in this world and look to its gifts and promises for the gratification of our desires, and place its riches, honours, and pleasures first in our list of treasures. Even after the truth has dawned upon us; yes, even after our eyes have looked upon Jesus and our hearts opened to His love and power, how easily are we drawn aside; how readily driven again, by the allurements of things visible, the faithlessness of our hearts and the strength of old habits, to the beggarly elements of the world; how constantly are we forgetting to seek *first* the kingdom of God and His righteousness, satisfied that He should bestow all other things upon us, as He deems needful and for our good. Take the great Scripture-text, "*where your treasure is, there shall your heart be also.*" *Brethren, where is your heart?*

God knows that wayward heart, and Christ our compassionate High-priest knows all the temptations which beset us here? And therefore we are not left alone; but by His Spirit, our Lord and Saviour is with us, always with us. He uses the experiences of our life to wean us from its idols, and lets us taste the bitter dregs of all its sweetened poisons, and suffer from the unquenched thirst, after having vainly applied at all its broken cisterns. He appeals to us in strains of entreaty or terror, to rouse us from our fall and draw us back from sin. And He surrounds us with tokens of His presence and proofs of His love and power, and with means of grace, which call us back to God, and help the feeble mind, and guide the faltering professor, and fix the heart on Him as its great treasure and train it for His favor and His presence.

This day we stand before Him, and He is nigh to hear our prayers. "Ask what I shall give thee." Ah, brethren, is there one among us, one of those who are invited to partake of this sacramental feast and revive in it the memory of His love, of all He did and suffered for us, all He bids us do; that would be willing to draw nigh, except with the desire for HIM and His presence and His grace; fo an understanding heart and obedient life?

Whenever we are called to partake of the blessed Sacrament of the Lord's Supper, we are called upon *to dedicate ourselves anew to Him.* By all the tokens of His love, by the hopes of His atoning death, the saving power of His resurrection, and His all-prevailing intercession, *to give our hearts to Him and live to His glory!* — It is for this purpose that Christ has instituted the Sacrament, and interrupts the easy tenor of our Christian life and our every-day routine, in which we are apt to forget our high and holy calling, by the silent appeals, but *appeals of irresistible love and of overwhelming solemnity*, which come to us, month by month, from this sacred table.

Every time we come up here, we virtually renew the baptismal vow, again plead before God the merits of Jesus as our only righteousness, again promise to renounce sin, the world and the devil, and to obey and serve God.

And, brethren, who that knows his own heart, and the many violations of the sacred compact which he has been guilty of, will not be moved, in the solemn consciousness of his unfitness, to pray God that now at last, after so many failings, he may have grace to keep that covenant more faithfully, and love and serve his Master better. We look back upon our former life and the many inconsistencies of which it convicts us, and the wayward desires which have interfered with the happiness, that belongs properly to the Christian and results only from perfect submission to God's will. We remember in sorrow— for we have suffered from them—the many delusions and false attractions with which this world abounds, and which but too often have proved a snare to us. We stand there once more as babes in Christ, as those who come as sinners and flee from destruction to Jesus. It is like taking again that decided step which every one takes when first coming to the Lord, to turn from the world to Him who has saved us, to turn from earth to heaven our promised home, to turn from everything that binds the heart in the service of sin, and say: "*What have I to do any more with idols?*"

What have *I* to do with idols? *I* who have been called by Christ, who have been saved by His blood, who have been made a member of Christ, a child of God, an inheritor of the kingdom of heaven? *I* who have been admitted to the sweet intercourse with my Master, and the communion with my Lord and King; who have felt His pardoning power and the constraining influence of His love? *I* who have sworn to be His faithful soldier and servant unto my life's end?

"*What have I to do any more with idols?*"

Ah, brethren, as we stand here, let us remember that His eye is upon us, the eye of the all-seeing Judge! Let us remember the exhortation: "to judge ourselves lest we be judged of the Lord," and "so to examine our own consciences, that we may come holy and clean to such a heavenly feast, in the marriage-garment required by God in holy Scripture and be received as worthy partakers of that holy table?" I know, we have all to labour for this, and to renew the resolution henceforth to have nothing more to do with idols. In our heart, which ought to be a temple of God—alas how apt we are to keep a niche filled with some other object of our worship? And as in the days of His flesh the Saviour drove from the temple all who desecrated it by worldly traffic—much more let us pray Him to make our heart clean and keep it as an holy temple and give us grace to say:

> The dearest idol I have known,
> Whate'er that idol be,
> Help me to tear it from Thy throne
> And worship only THEE!

Come forth, ye idols of my wicked heart, and yield your place to its rightful owner! Fall down, like Dagon's image at the presence of the Highest, and let my Saviour take possession of His blood-bought treasure! *Ye darling sins* that have long kept me from Jesus, that have led me captive against my will and caused me to deny the Lord who bought me. *This day*, by the grace of God, I resolve to leave you all for Jesus. " *What have I to do any more with idols?* " even should they be dear as a right hand or a right eye?

Ye unlawful attachments; ye affections that, lawful in themselves, become idolatrous, because they are not subordinate to the supreme object of my love: loose your hold and set me free! This day, by the grace of God, I resolve not to degrade the dearest relationships of life by making them sinful, but to love father, mother, sister, brother, wife and child and country better, by loving them in the Lord.

Ye earthly pleasures, the smiling, dazzling idol with its ten thousand worshippers and its unhallowed temples all around me, I renounce your passing joys, and crown of fading flowers, for the cross of Christ, the crown of life! Mine be the joy in the Holy Ghost, mine the pleasures which are at God's right hand forever more. "*What have I to do any more with idols?*"

Thou ruling demon of the age, thou fondly cherished idol, *mammon*, love of money, gloating over the glittering gold and the goods that perish in the using and buying souls, immortal souls for pelf: behold, this day I consecrate myself, my strength, my wealth, my all, to God! to be His steward, His almoner, His servant—I cannot serve two masters. *"What have I to do any more with idols?"*

Fear of men, that keeps the young from Christ and from secret prayer, that keeps the father from worshipping God in his family, that keeps so many from confessing Christ; that keeps the best of us so often from freely, resolutely doing what is right, what God and conscience approve! I have felt God's love and spirit now, I will not be afraid of a man that shall die, I will no longer fear those who only have power over the body, I will fear God and keep His commandments. *"What have I to do any more with idols?"*

Ambition! God forbid that I should glory, save in the cross of Christ, my Lord, by whom this world is crucified to me and I unto the world.

> Make me little and unknown,
> Loved and prized by Thee alone!

Self-righteousnesss! From this day I seek not my own righteousness, which is of the law, but that which is through the faith of Christ; the righteousness which is of God by faith. This day I will rejoice that Christ Jesus came into the world to save sinners, of whom I am chief; and thank God that "to whom much is forgiven, the same loveth much!"

Brethren, whatever the past may have been, however much we may have been enslaved by the power of sin, or the allurements of the world, or kept from Jesus by the spirit of legality; the time past of our life ought to suffice us to have wrought their will. *The Deliverer has come*, comes to us to-day and bids us no longer to live the rest of our life in the flesh to the lusts of men, but to the will of God. Whatever obstacles the love, or at least the influence of these idols may have thrown in our path, *to-day* we are solemnly called upon to renounce them. *To-day* the tokens of grace and mercy teach us to exclaim:

> "Thy love unknown
> Has broken every barrier down.
> Now to be Thine, yea Thine alone,
> O Lamb of God, I come!

This, brethren, is indeed the burden of to-day's solemnity. Only when coming in this spirit and with this resolution, and with the cry for help that He would give us this mind and keep us steadfast in this purpose—can we be worthy recipients of these holy mysteries. We can never come, because we have not sinned, because our faith and good works have made us worthy; but we cannot come either, whilst willingly remaining the servants of sin and the victims of such idols. *We must come now and ever with the prayer, " make us a clean heart, and renew a right spirit within us !"*

But, is not this too the day and the opportunity to *create* in us this holy desire, and *enable us to form these holy resolutions?* Here is gathered before us all that can move the heart. *The past* stands before us in the sacramented memorial of all that Christ has done for us, and teaches us "that God so loved the world, that He gave His Only Begotten Son, that whosoever believeth in Him should not perish, but have everlasting life," and that "there is no condemnation to them that are in Christ Jesus." *The present* is fragrant with the dews of heaven, that descend upon the heart in every ordinance of Christ, and teach us, that now exalted to the right hand of power, our Saviour has not forsaken us, but still carries on the work of our redemption, "continually making intercession for us!" *The future* is here radiant with its glorious promises in Christ. This humble feast is but the type of our full communion with Him in heaven. It gives us the assurance of our final victory, and lifts the heart in faith to behold the Saviour coming again in power and great glory to call us to the home above, and to the marriage feast of heaven!

Oh, brethren, here is our God—*Jesus Christ.*

The same yesterday, when He died that we might live.

The same to-day, when He liveth to make intercession for us.

The same forever, when He shall come again to take us into His glory.

WHAT HAVE WE TO DO ANY MORE WITH IDOLS?

www.ingramcontent.com/pod-product-compliance
Lightning Source LLC
Chambersburg PA
CBHW022023240426
43667CB00042B/1063